Practice with Prefixes

Antarctic

bicycle

submarine

Authors

Timothy Rasinski, Ph.D.

Nancy Padak, Ed.D.

Rick M. Newton, Ph.D.

Evengeline Newton, Ph.D.

SHELL EDUCATION

Publishing Credits

Dona Herweck Rice, *Editor-in-Chief*; Robin Erickson, *Production Director*;
Lee Aucoin, *Creative Director*; Timothy J. Bradley, *Illustration Manager*;
Sara Johnson M.S.Ed, *Senior Editor*; Evelyn Garcia, *Associate Education Editor*;
Leah Quillian, *Assistant Editor*; Grace Alba, *Designer*;
Corinne Burton, *M.A.Ed., Publisher*

Standard
© 2004 Mid-continent Research for Education and Learning (McREL)

Shell Education
5301 Oceanus Drive
Huntington Beach, CA 92649-1030
http://www.shelleducation.com
ISBN 978-1-4258-0882-2
©2012 Shell Educational Publishing, Inc.

Table of Contents

Why Roots? Vocabulary Research and Practice

What Is a Root?

A *root* is a word part that contains meaning (and not merely sound). There are three categories of roots, depending on their placement within a word:

- **prefix:** a root at the beginning of a word. For example, in the word *retraction*, the initial *re-* is a prefix, meaning "back, again."

- **base:** the core root, which provides a word with its basic meaning. In the word *retraction*, the base is *tract*, which means "pull, draw, drag."

- **suffix:** a root that ends a word. In the word *retraction*, the final *–ion* is a suffix, meaning "act of, state of."

What Do Prefixes Do?

A prefix serves one of three functions:

- A prefix can *negate* a word by meaning "not." The most common negating prefixes are *un-* (e.g., *unhappy, unwashed*) and negative *in-, im-, il-* (e.g., *invisible, impossible, illegal*). Some directional prefixes can also be negating. For example, the prefix variations *di-, dis-, dif-*, which mean "apart, in different directions," can also mean "not." Examples: things that are "not similar" are *dissimilar;* a *difficult* task is "not" easy.

- A prefix can be *directional.* This is the most common function of a prefix: it sends the base of the word in a specific direction. For example, the prefix *ex-* means "out," *re-* means "back, again," *sub-* means "under, below," and *ad-* means "to, toward, add to." For example, an *exit* sign indicates the way "out" of a building; we *descend* a staircase when we go "down"; when class *convenes*, it comes "together"; when class is *dismissed*, students scatter "in different directions"; when they *proceed* to their buses, they move "forward, ahead" to their bus stops.

Thus, using the base *tract-* (pull, draw, drag), *extract* means to "pull out" (e.g., we *extract* a tooth); *retract* means to "take or pull back" (e.g., a journalist *retracts* a statement; a cat *retracts* its claws); *subtract* means to "take a lower number from a higher one"; to *attract* means to "pull, draw someone to or toward an object" (the prefix *at-* in this word is assimilated *ad-*; e.g., a magnet *attracts* metal objects, which are "pulled toward" it).

> **Note:** Although students may not be aware that prefixes can suggest direction, they can benefit from examining the prefix and thinking about the direction of these words (both literal and metaphorical).

- A prefix can have *intensifying* force, meaning "very, thoroughly." Some directional prefixes may also be intensifying. For example, the prefix *per-*, meaning "through" (as in *permeate, perforate, percolate*), can also mean "very" or "thoroughly": a *perfectly* baked cake, for example, is "thoroughly" done.

- This book presents negating prefixes, directional prefixes, and numerical-quantitative prefixes with intensifying force.

Why Roots? Vocabulary Research and Practice *(cont.)*

What Is Assimilation?

Some prefixes have multiple forms as shown in the chart on page 8. These slight changes reflect an easily recognizable and predictable phenomenon called *assimilation.* Assimilation simply means that some consonants at the beginning of a word change and become like ("similar to" = *assimilate*) the consonants that follow them.

It is obvious that the prefix *con-*, for example, occurs in the words *convention* and *conference.* Through assimilation, a variation of *con-* also appears in *collect, commotion,* and *correct.* The reason is simple: assimilation makes a word easier to pronounce (consider *conlect* vs. *collect*).

The concept of assimilation can be easily understood and presented in a 3-step approach. The 3 steps are: (1) unassimilated prefixes (i.e., the prefix is not changed since it is easily pronounced with the next letter of the word), as in *convention, invent, advent, subterranean*; (2) *partial assimilation* (i.e., the prefix changes its final *n-* into an *m-* to facilitate pronunciation with the next letter of the word), as in *compose, imbibe, import*; and (3) *full assimilation* (i.e., the prefix changes its final consonant into the same consonant as the next letter of the word, to facilitate pronunciation), which results in a doubled consonant, as in *collect, illegal, attract, suffer, support.*

Unassimilated prefixes thus retain their original form as *con-, in-, ad-, sub-*, and so on. *Partial assimilation* occurs when prefixes that end in *n-* (*con-, in-*) change to *m-* before bases that begin with *b-* or *p-*: *con + bine* becomes *combine*, for example.

Full assimilation occurs when the final consonant of the prefix is dropped and the following consonant doubled: *con + lect* becomes *collect*, and *ad + tract* becomes *attract*.

Although assimilation causes spelling changes, the meaning of the prefix does not change. The Teaching Tips for each lesson will let you know if the prefix you are teaching can undergo assimilation.

To teach assimilation, explain the concept to students by showing them a few examples, such as the ones provided in the chart (page 8). As you discuss these examples, be sure that students recognize the prefix of the word. Tell them that whenever a doubled consonant appears near the beginning of a word, they should divide the word between the doubled consonant and identify the assimilated prefix. Also, remind them that *con-* and *in-* may partially assimilate and become *com-* or *im-* when they attach to bases that begin with *b-* or *p-*.

See the following page for an outline of the 3-step approach to presenting assimilation. This approach uses examples of commonly-known words which can be helpful when introducing the concept. In each step, ask students to pronounce the prefix and base separately. Then, ask them to pronounce the prefix and the base together as a single word. In Step 1, pronunciation is easy without altering the prefix. In Step 2, partial assimilation makes the prefix easier to pronounce with the base. In Step 3, full assimilation is required to make the prefix easier to pronounce, resulting in a double consonant near the beginning of the word.

Why Roots? Vocabulary Research and Practice (cont.)

What Is Assimilation? (cont.)

Step 1: Unassimilated Prefixes

con + vention = convention

in + visible = invisible

sub + terranean = subterranean

ob + struction = obstruction

ex + pose = expose

dis + tract = distract

> **Note:** We can easily pronounce the unaltered prefix with the base. Hence, there is no need to assimilate.

Step 2: Partial Assimilation

in + possible = impossible

con + pose = compose

con + bine = combine

con + fort = comfort

> **Note:** We cannot easily pronounce *n* when it is followed by such consonants as *b*, *p*, and (occasionally) *f*. In such cases, the final *n* of the prefix partially assimilates into *m*.

Step 3: Full Assimilation

con + rect = correct

in + legal = illegal

sub + fer = suffer

ob + pose = oppose

ex + fect = effect

dis + fer = differ

ad + similation = assimilation

> **Note:** We cannot easily pronounce these unaltered prefixes when followed by certain consonants. In such cases, the final consonant of the prefix changes into the initial consonant of the base that follows it. The result is a doubled consonant near the beginning.

Why Roots? Vocabulary Research and Practice (cont.)

Latin Prefixes that Assimilate

Prefix	Meaning	Examples
ad-	to, toward, add to	*admit, accelerate, affect, aggravate, allusion, appendix, arrogant, assimilate, attract*
con-, co-	with, together, very	*congregate, coworker, collect, combine, commit, compose, correct*
ex-, e-, ef-	out, from, completely	*expose, edict, effect*
dis-, di-, dif-	apart, in different directions, not	*disintegrate, divert, different, difficult*
in-, im-, il- (directional)	in, on, into, against	*induct, insert, imbibe, immigrant, import, impose, illustrate*
in-, im-, il- (negative)	not	*infinite, insatiable, ignoble, illegal, illegible, impossible, irresponsible*
ob-	toward, up against, completely	*obstruct, occurrence, offensive, oppose*
sub-	under, up from under	*submarine, succeed, suffer, support, suspend*

Why Teach with a Roots Approach?

Teaching with a roots approach is efficient. Over 60 percent of the words students encounter in their reading have recognizable word parts (Nagy, Anderson, Schommer, Scott, and Stallman 1989). Moreover, content-area vocabulary is largely of Greek and Latin origin (Harmon, Hedrick, and Wood 2005). Many words from Greek and Latin roots meet the criteria for "tier two" words and are appropriate for instruction (Beck, McKeown, and Kucan 2002).

Root study also promotes independent word learning (Carlisle 2010). In addition, students learn to make connections among words that are semantically related (Nagy and Scott 2000). Research suggests that the brain is a pattern detector (Cunningham 2004). Latin and Greek word roots follow linguistic patterns that can help students with the meaning, sound, and spelling of English words. Indeed, Latin and Greek roots have consistent orthographic (spelling) patterns (Rasinski and Padak 2008; Bear, Invernizzi, Templeton, and Johnston 2007).

Young readers' word instruction is often characterized by a study of word patterns called *rimes*. A Latin-Greek roots approach is the next logical and developmental step in word learning (Bear, Invernizzi, Templeton, and Johnston 2007). Many English language learners speak first languages semantically related to Latin (e.g., Spanish, which is a "Romance" [Latin-derived] language). Enhancing this natural linguistic connection can accelerate these students' vocabulary growth (Blachowicz, Fisher, Ogle, and Watts-Taffe 2006).

Many states are beginning to include a study of derivations in their elementary and middle school literacy standards.

What Does Research Say About Using a Roots Approach?

The size and depth of elementary students' vocabulary is associated with proficiency in reading comprehension. Effective vocabulary instruction results in higher levels of reading comprehension (Baumann et al. 2002; Beck, Perfetti, and McKeown 1982; Kame'enui, Carnine, and Freschi 1982; Stahl and Fairbanks 1986).

Morphological analysis (e.g., via a roots approach) is important because it is generative and allows students to make connections among semantically related words or word families (Nagy and Scott 2000). In fact, developing morphological awareness is an integral component of word learning for young children (Biemiller and Slonim 2001). In a comprehensive review of 16 studies analyzing the effect of instruction in morphological awareness on literacy achievement, Carlisle (2010) observes that "children learn morphemes as they learn language" (465).

Classroom-based studies have demonstrated the effectiveness of teaching word parts and context clues (Baumann et al. 2005) in the primary (Biemiller 2005; Mountain 2005; Porter-Collier 2010) and intermediate grades (Baumann et al. 2002; Carlisle 2000; Kieffer and Lesaux 2007). Research in content-area vocabulary has demonstrated the effectiveness of teaching Greek and Latin word roots, especially for struggling readers (Harmon et al. 2005).

No single instructional method is sufficient. Teachers need a variety of methods that teach word meanings while also increasing the depth of word knowledge (Blachowicz et al. 2006; Lehr, Osborn, and Hiebert 2007). These methods should aim at the following:

- **Immersion.** Students need frequent opportunities to use new words in diverse oral and print contexts in order to learn them thoroughly (Blachowicz and Fisher 2006).

- **Metacognitive and metalinguistic awareness.** Students must understand and know how to manipulate the structural features of language (Nagy and Scott 2000).

- **Word consciousness (e.g., an awareness of and interest in words)** (Graves and Watts-Taffe 2002). Word exploration (etymology) and word play (puns, riddles) are central to vocabulary development (Lehr et al. 2007).

Differentiating Instruction

To make *Practice with Prefixes* most effective, you may want to differentiate instruction for students who have particular needs. Groups of students who may benefit from differentiated instruction include English language learners, struggling readers, above-level readers, and students with special needs. The sections below offer some instructional suggestions for each group of students.

Supporting English Language Learners

Like their peers, English language learners benefit from the focus on meaning using research-based strategies to learn new roots and words. Frequent opportunities to try new words out in a variety of contexts will help English language learners, as will partner or small-group work, which has the additional advantage of supporting English language learners' conversational English.

Especially if students' native languages derive from Latin (e.g., Spanish), make comparisons to the native languages whenever possible. When they learn to look for roots within words, Spanish speakers will be able to relate many word roots in English to their counterparts in Spanish. Sharing their knowledge with other classmates will help everyone grow.

You may need to provide additional time for English language learners to complete activities. You may also need to add context to activities, to make certain that new words appear in the context of sentences. For example, you (or a tutor or peer) can read sentences aloud to these students, then ask them to read the sentences with you, and finally invite independent responses.

Concrete context will also support English language learners' work with prefixes and words. You can use gestures or body language to provide nonlinguistic support when possible. You can also provide (or ask students to make) word cards for students to manipulate or word banks with answers for students to select from.

Supporting Struggling Readers

Struggling readers will benefit from extra support and instructional time. You may want to do a few examples with them before encouraging independent response. Making activities more concrete and providing word banks for answers will also help. Students might work with partners to complete activities. You will want to monitor struggling readers' progress and make adjustments as needed.

Differentiating Instruction (cont.)

Supporting Above-Level Readers

Above-level readers may not need all the examples provided in lessons to understand the concepts being taught. You may want to have students complete only the most challenging examples. Often, above-level readers will enjoy additional challenges. You may want them to develop their own activities using prefixes for others to complete. The Internet offers tools for making crossword puzzles and other word games that students may develop themselves to challenge their peers (e.g., **http://www.puzzlemaker.com**).

Above-level students may be interested in peer tutoring as well. They may also lead efforts to find words using the prefixes of focus in other texts. However, it is important to ensure that the extra challenges you provide are more fun than the busywork.

Response to Intervention

Response to Intervention (RTI) is an approach to instructional delivery for students who struggle with or have special needs in some aspect of learning (National Association of State Directors of Education 2006). The RTI model has three levels of intensity. The first level or tier is for the majority (about 75–80 percent) of students who benefit from universal instruction. The second level or tier is for a smaller percentage (10–15 percent) of students in a classroom; these students need more targeted instruction because universal instruction does not enable them to be successful. This instruction typically involves adaptations that a general education teacher can reasonably accomplish (Fuchs and Fuchs 1998), such as providing extra time, additional lessons, extra instructional materials such as concrete visual scaffolds, or other adjustments in support. The third level or tier includes the smallest percentage (5–10 percent) of students—those who do not respond sufficiently to Tier II instruction and who likely need to be screened for special education placement.

The following are some ideas for using the RTI model to differentiate instruction with *Practice with Prefixes*:

- **Tier I:** Encourage peer work. Students who are above level may need additional challenges.

- **Tier II:** Arrange peer work. If possible, provide instruction in small groups and increase instructional time. Monitor progress more frequently than Tier I. Provide additional practice. Involve parents. Encourage use of graphics (e.g., word webs) and pictorial representations (e.g., have students make prefix word cards with words on one side and sketches on the other. These can be used to play word games or as independent study aids).

- **Tier III:** Coordinate with the student's tutor or special education teacher. Allow extra time. Provide extra opportunities for practice and review. Individual instruction may be needed. Monitor progress more often than Tier II.

How to Use This Book

This introductory section of *Practice with Prefixes* presents management, research, and background information to orient you to a roots approach. *Practice with Prefixes* is a stand-alone resource book for teachers and students that presents the most frequently encountered Latin prefixes in English. It also presents introductory Greek prefixes. Each lesson provides content explanations, instructional guidelines, and student activities necessary to teach prefixes and help learners understand how to "dissect" (Divide and Conquer) and "compose" (Combine and Create) words from everyday and academic vocabulary. Suggestions for extension activities and assessment are also included.

Five instructional units present five lessons each followed by a Review Page (suitable for assessment) on specific prefixes. The prefixes begin at the easiest/most frequently encountered level (Units I and II), progress to the intermediate level of directional prefixes and word difficulty (Units III and IV), and culminate in "number and quantitative prefixes" from both Greek and Latin (Unit V).

Instructional Planning

Before beginning to teach with *Practice with Prefixes*, read the introductory material and skim several lessons. Then, decide how to incorporate the lessons within your reading/language arts curriculum:

- How many minutes per day can you devote to the lessons?

- How often can you teach them during the week?

- At what time of day will you and your students practice with prefixes?

- Glance at the Review Page at the end of each unit, which can be used for assessment.

How to Use This Book (cont.)

The information in this book is cumulative but not sequential. Depending on your students, you may begin at any point. The following is an outline of each unit:

About Unit I

Unit I introduces students to the skill of dividing and conquering vocabulary.

Lessons 1 and 2 present easy and familiar compound words. By dividing compound words into component parts, students learn to look inside a word for its semantic units (i.e., parts that have meaning and not merely sound).

Lessons 3 and 4 continue to build on the skill of looking inside a word for its semantic unit while focusing on the negating prefixes *un-* and *in-*.

Lesson 5 introduces the concept of assimilation: the prefix *in-*, ending in a consonant, changes into *im-* or *il-*, depending on the following consonant in the word (e.g., *impossible*, *illegal*).

All the sample words in Lessons 3–5 present prefixes attached to intact words. Students will learn how to negate an existing word as well as learn how to detach a negating prefix and recognize the original word.

The Combine and Create activities and the Read and Reason passages present the prefixes and words in larger contexts. The unit ends with a one-page review exercise suitable for assessment.

About Unit II

Unit II presents five of the most essential Latin directional prefixes in the English vocabulary and builds on the Divide and Conquer skills introduced in Unit I.

Lessons 6 and 7 present the prefixes *re-* ("back, again") and *pre-* ("before"), which attach to intact words and to Latin bases. They form many words that students either already know or will readily recognize.

Lesson 8 presents the prefixes *ex-*, *e-*, and *ef-* meaning "out," and Lesson 9 presents *sub-*, meaning "below, under." Assimilated forms of *sub-*, such as *sup-*, *suf-*, and *suc-*, appear in such words as *support* (to carry or bear up from "under"), *suffer* (to endure from "below, under"), and *succeed* (to move up from "under" and accomplish).

Lesson 10 presents the prefixes *co-* and *con-*, explaining that the form *co-* frequently attaches to intact words (e.g., *coauthor*, *costar*, *coworker*) and that *con-* attaches to many Latin bases (e.g., *convert*, *conduct*, *contact*).

The Combine and Create activities as well as Read and Reason passages present the prefixes and words in larger contexts. The unit ends with a one-page review exercise, suitable for assessment.

How to Use This Book (cont.)

About Unit III

Unit III presents more of the most useful directional prefixes. Lesson 11 presents "directional" *in-* and its assimilated forms, *im-* and *il-*. These prefixes appear in many words that students already know and in words that may be new to them. Students receive practice in distinguishing negative *in-*, *im-*, *il-* words (e.g., *invisible, impossible, illegal*) from directional *in-*, *im-*, *il-* words (e.g., *induct, import, illuminate*).

Lesson 12 presents *com-*, *col-*, the assimilated forms of the prefix *co-*, *con-* (which are introduced in Unit II, Lesson 10). This prefix means "with, together" and appears in such words as *collect, compose*, and *combine*.

Lesson 13 presents *de-*, meaning "down, off of," in such everyday words as *defrost* and in academic words like *descend, decapitate*, and *demotion*.

Lesson 14 follows with *pro-*, meaning "forward, ahead, for," which students will readily recognize in such words as *promotion, proceed, progress* and in such hyphenated words as *pro-war* and *pro-environment*.

Lesson 15 presents the prefixes *tra-* and *trans-*, meaning "across, change," which appears in many words from academic vocabulary, such as *transformation, transportation*, and *traverse*.

In Divide and Conquer, students are also informally introduced to a number of useful Latin bases to which these prefixes attach. The Combine and Create activities as well as Read and Reason passages present the prefixes and words in larger contexts.

About Unit IV

Unit IV presents intermediate-level prefixes that appear in everyday words, in academic vocabulary, and in the content areas.

Lesson 16 presents *inter-*, meaning "between, among," which appears in words that students already know, such as *interactive, Internet*, and *interrupt*. This prefix also appears in words from social studies (e.g., *international, interstate, interregnum, interrogate*).

Lesson 17 presents the prefix *dis-* and its variant forms *di-* and *dif-*, meaning "apart, in different directions, not." The prefix appears in many academic words that refer to literal or figurative "scattering" (e.g., when class is *dismissed,* students physically scatter "in different directions"; but when we are *distracted* by noise in the hallway, we are figuratively drawn "apart" from our concentration). The prefix *dis-* can also negate whole words (e.g., *disqualify, disability, disinfect, dissimilar*).

Lesson 18 presents *a-*, *ab- abs-*, meaning "away, from, away from." This prefix indicates both the physical direction of "away" (as in *abducting* a kidnap victim and *averting* one's eyes) and the figurative sense of "away" (in words like *abstract, aversion, abstain*).

Lesson 19 follows with *super-*, *sur*, meaning "on top of, over, above." Words beginning with these prefixes refer to the physical, literal direction of "above, over" (e.g., to *superimpose* a bowl over a plate; to *survey* land by looking "over" the terrain with a raised tripod) and to being "above" others in rank or degree (e.g., a *supervisor* "oversees" subordinate workers).

How to Use This Book (cont.)

About Unit IV (cont.)

Lesson 20 presents the prefix *ad-*, meaning "to, toward, add to," and its assimilating forms. This is the most frequently assimilated of all Latin prefixes, accounting for the doubling of a consonant after initial *a-* in nearly all English words. In fact, the word *assimilation* itself begins with *assimilated ad-* (ad + simulation = *assimilation*, the making of one consonant "similar" "to" another). Students receive practice in recognizing this prefix in such words as *accelerate, affect, alliteration, aggravate*, and *alleviate*.

About Unit V

Unit V presents some of the most frequent numerical and quantifying prefixes in English.

Lessons 21, 22, and 23 present the Latin prefixes for the numbers 1, 2, 3, 4, 10, 100, and 1,000. The numerical prefixes *uni-* and *unit-*, presented in Lesson 21, appear in many words that students readily recognize as meaning "one": a *unicorn* has "one" horn; a *unicycle* has "one" wheel. But this prefix appears in other words that students may never have thought about as meaning "one": a *uniform* is a "single" "form" of clothing worn by many people; a *unique* person is "one of a kind, singular."

Lesson 22 presents the numerical prefixes for "two" and "three," *bi-* and *tri-*. In addition to appearing in common words (e.g., *bicycle, triangle*), these prefixes appear in specialized academic words (e.g., *bilateral agreements, bicameral congress, trisected angles*).

Lesson 23 presents prefixes essential for mathematic skills: "four" *quarts* in a gallon and "four" feet on a *quadruped*; a *decimal* point indicates "$\frac{1}{10}$," a *century* is a period of 100 years, and a *millennium* lasts 1,000 years. These numerical prefixes are found in mathematics, science (e.g., *centimeter, millimeter, milligrams)*, and social studies (e.g., *bicentennial celebration, quadrennial elections*).

Lessons 24 and 25 present Greek and Latin prefixes of size and quantity. Lesson 24 presents Latin *multi-*, meaning "many," which appears in academic words (e.g., a *multilingual* person speaks "many" "languages"; a *multilateral* agreement reflects the "many" "sides" of the parties agreeing to it).

Lesson 24 also presents the Greek prefix *poly-*, which means "much, many" in such academic words as *polytheist* (one who believes in "many" "gods") and *polygon* (a geometric figure with "many" "angles" and sides).

Lesson 25 presents Latin *magn(i)-*, meaning "big, large," in such words as *magnify* (to enlarge, "make" "big"), *magnitude* (a "large" scope), *magnate* (a "big" or major figure in business), and *magnanimous* (generous and "large" "hearted"). The same lesson presents the Greek prefix *mega-, megalo-*, meaning "big, large" (e.g., *megalomania*) and Greek *micro-*, meaning "small" (e.g., *microscope, microcosm*).

All of the units end with a one-page review exercise suitable for assessment.

How to Use This Book *(cont.)*

Lesson Overview

Each lesson begins with **Teaching Tips** that provide essential information about the prefix. Reading this section before you teach the lesson will provide you with a foundation to ensure student success.

The **Guided Practice** portion of each lesson includes suggestions for **Activating Background Knowledge** about the prefix. These suggestions provide interactive teaching strategies to help elicit what students already know and to build on that foundation.

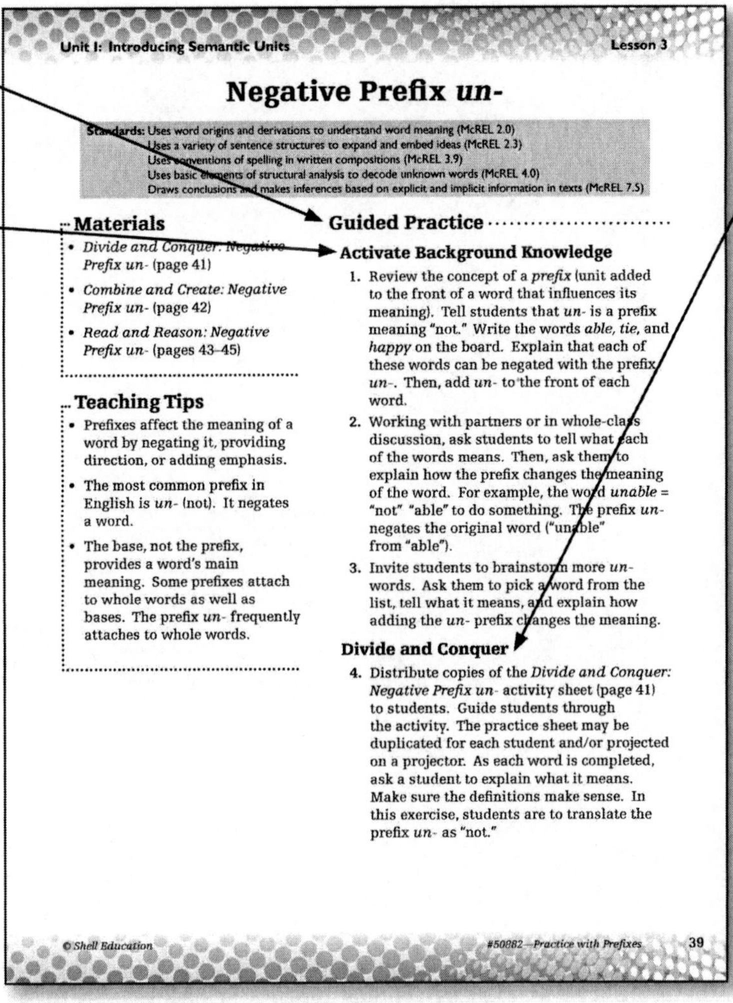
Unit I: Introducing Semantic Units — Lesson 3

Negative Prefix *un-*

Standards: Uses word origins and derivations to understand word meaning (McREL 2.0)
Uses a variety of sentence structures to expand and embed ideas (McREL 2.3)
Uses conventions of spelling in written compositions (McREL 3.9)
Uses basic elements of structural analysis to decode unknown words (McREL 4.0)
Draws conclusions and makes inferences based on explicit and implicit information in texts (McREL 7.5)

Materials

- *Divide and Conquer: Negative Prefix un-* (page 41)
- *Combine and Create: Negative Prefix un-* (page 42)
- *Read and Reason: Negative Prefix un-* (pages 43–45)

Teaching Tips

- Prefixes affect the meaning of a word by negating it, providing direction, or adding emphasis.
- The most common prefix in English is *un-* (not). It negates a word.
- The base, not the prefix, provides a word's main meaning. Some prefixes attach to whole words as well as bases. The prefix *un-* frequently attaches to whole words.

Guided Practice

Activate Background Knowledge

1. Review the concept of a *prefix* (unit added to the front of a word that influences its meaning). Tell students that *un-* is a prefix meaning "not." Write the words *able, tie,* and *happy* on the board. Explain that each of these words can be negated with the prefix *un-*. Then, add *un-* to the front of each word.
2. Working with partners or in whole-class discussion, ask students to tell what each of the words means. Then, ask them to explain how the prefix changes the meaning of the word. For example, the word *unable* = "not" "able" to do something. The prefix *un-* negates the original word ("unable" from "able").
3. Invite students to brainstorm more *un-* words. Ask them to pick a word from the list, tell what it means, and explain how adding the *un-* prefix changes the meaning.

Divide and Conquer

4. Distribute copies of the *Divide and Conquer: Negative Prefix un-* activity sheet (page 41) to students. Guide students through the activity. The practice sheet may be duplicated for each student and/or projected on a projector. As each word is completed, ask a student to explain what it means. Make sure the definitions make sense. In this exercise, students are to translate the prefix *un-* as "not."

© Shell Education — #50882—Practice with Prefixes — 39

Then students are presented with a word list called **Divide and Conquer**. Each word includes the prefix that is the focus of the lesson. The prefixes are attached to both intact English words and to Latin bases, whose meaning is provided. As students "translate" the prefix and the base word, they study the meaning of each semantic unit and identify the definition from the Answer Bank. This activity helps students understand how to extract meaning using roots.

How to Use This Book (cont.)

Lesson Overview (cont.)

The **Combine and Create** activity of each lesson teaches students to combine word parts in order to use words in written and oral academic work. In these activities, students combine word parts (prefixes and bases) to generate vocabulary, and they also examine context clues (for words in phrases and textbook settings, including short composition sentences) to determine correct responses. As students complete and review their answers, they share the words and sentences they have made with classmates, because using and hearing new words is an important part of learning them.

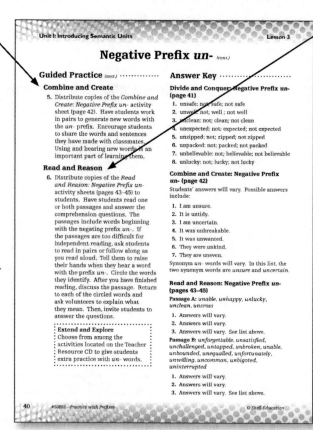

Two **Read and Reason** activities follow one at an easy-readability-level and one more challenging. You may choose one or both of these passages, which contain several words using the prefix of the lesson. As students read to themselves or listen to the teacher reading aloud, they identify the prefix words in extended texts that center on a wide range of interesting topics.

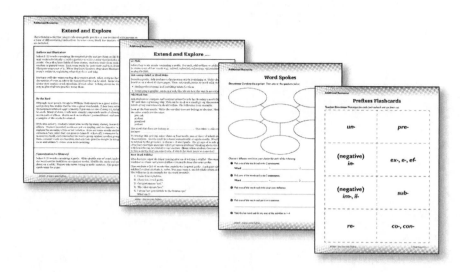

If additional practice is needed or desired, you may use the **Extension Activities** found on the Teacher Resource CD.

How to Use This Book (cont.)

Tips for Implementation

In this section, we offer some general implementation tips as well as extension ideas.

General Tips

As you plan, keep instructional goals and learning outcomes in mind. Develop regular routines for vocabulary instruction and practice. Read the **Teaching Tips** before beginning each lesson.

Some teachers have noticed a "learning curve" when their students begin working from a roots approach, perhaps because students are accustomed to memorizing only as a word-learning strategy. Be patient with your students while they are experiencing this learning curve; provide extra support if needed (e.g., invite students to work in pairs).

When you introduce a new prefix, do the dividing and conquering with students before asking them to work independently. Encourage students to work with partners so they can talk through the process. Also, find time for students to explore words with others.

When discussing answers, use the definition of the root in your talk (e.g., *replay* means "play again"). You can also reword key sentences substituting the root meaning for the word. Remember to keep the focus on the meanings of the prefixes and not on memorizing particular words.

If students have questions about words that you cannot answer, you can say, "I'm not sure. Let's look it up." Then show students how to consult a resource to find the answer. Do not shy away from using this option. It is important for students to understand that word learning is a lifelong process and that teachers are learners, too. Moreover, these situations provide authentic opportunities to teach students how to use reference books and websites.

Above all, we urge you to create a classroom setting that stimulates word curiosity and exploration. Consider using the prefix you are teaching as a "Prefix of the Week." Encourage students to search for words that share the prefix and add them to a list you have prominently displayed. Whenever possible, encourage playful activities where students can explore words with the prefix they are studying. Such activities can often be quick and spontaneous. If you have a few extra moments, try Twenty Questions or play Hangman with a word that uses the prefix students are learning.

Extension Possibilities

Students might use some activities in learning centers, work stations, or as homework. The **Combine and Create** and **Read and Reason** sections of each lesson may work especially well for this purpose.

Make word walls featuring prefixes you are studying. Invite students to look for words containing the prefix to add to the word wall. Challenge students to use words containing the prefix of focus in their writing (and oral language as well).

Ask students to review their previous writing for examples of words with the prefix of focus. These could be placed on a large sheet of chart paper or added to the word wall.

Challenge students to use words with prefixes in their content-area study. They can look for words containing a prefix in their reading and, perhaps, post these on chart paper. If enough words are accumulated, students can develop webs showing how the words relate to the content-area topic of study.

Correlation to Standards

Shell Education is committed to producing educational materials that are research and standards based. In this effort, we have correlated all of our products to the academic standards of all 50 United States, the District of Columbia, the Department of Defense Dependent Schools, and all Canadian provinces. We have also correlated to the Common Core State Standards.

How to Find Standards Correlations

To print a customized correlation report of this product for your state, visit our website at **http://www.shelleducation.com** and follow the on-screen directions. If you require assistance in printing correlation reports, please contact Customer Service at 1-800-858-7339.

Purpose and Intent of Standards

Legislation mandates that all states adopt academic standards that identify the skills students will learn in kindergarten through grade twelve. Many states also have standards for Pre-K. This same legislation sets requirements to ensure the standards are detailed and comprehensive.

Standards are designed to focus instruction and guide adoption of curricula. Standards are statements that describe the criteria necessary for students to meet specific academic goals. They define the knowledge, skills, and content students should acquire at each level. Standards are also used to develop standardized tests to evaluate students' academic progress.

Teachers are required to demonstrate how their lessons meet state standards. State standards are used in development of all of our products, so educators can be assured they meet the academic requirements of each state.

McREL Compendium

We use the Mid-continent Research for Education and Learning (McREL) Compendium to create standards correlations. Each year, McREL analyzes state standards and revises the compendium. By following this procedure, McREL is able to produce a general compilation of national standards. Each lesson in this product is based on one or more McREL standards. The chart on the following page lists each standard taught in this product and the page numbers for the corresponding lessons.

Correlation to Standards *(cont.)*

Standard	Page(s)
2.0—Uses word origins and derivations to understand word meaning	24, 31, 39, 46, 54, 63, 71, 79, 87, 95, 104, 112, 120, 128, 136, 146, 155, 164, 172, 180, 190, 198, 206, 215, 223
2.3—Uses a variety of sentence structures to expand and embed ideas	24, 31, 39, 46, 54, 63, 71, 79, 87, 95, 104, 112, 120, 128, 136, 146, 155, 164, 172, 180, 190, 198, 206, 215, 223
3.9—Uses conventions of spelling in written compositions	24, 31, 39, 46, 54, 63, 71, 79, 87, 95, 104, 112, 120, 128, 136, 146, 155, 164, 172, 180, 190, 198, 206, 215, 223
4.0—Uses basic elements of structural analysis to decode unknown words	24, 31, 39, 46, 54, 63, 71, 79, 87, 95, 104, 112, 120, 128, 136, 146, 155, 164, 172, 180, 190, 198, 206, 215, 223
7.5—Draws conclusions and makes inferences based on explicit and implicit information in texts	24, 31, 39, 46, 54, 63, 71, 79, 87, 95, 104, 112, 120, 128, 136, 146, 155, 164, 172, 180, 190, 198, 206, 215, 223

© *Shell Education*   #50882—*Practice with Prefixes*   **21**

About the Authors

Timothy Rasinski, Ph.D., is a professor of literacy education at Kent State University. He has written over 150 articles and has authored, coauthored, or edited over 15 books and curriculum programs on reading education. His research on reading has been cited by the National Reading Panel and has been published in journals such as *Reading Research Quarterly, The Reading Teacher, Reading Psychology*, and *The Journal of Educational Research*. Tim served on the Board of Directors of the International Reading Association, and from 1992–1999, he was coeditor of *The Reading Teacher*, the world's most widely read journal of literacy education. He has also served as editor of the *Journal of Literacy Research*, one of the premier research journals in reading. Tim is a past president of the College Reading Association, and he has won the A.B. Herr Award from the College Reading Association for his scholarly contributions to literacy education.

Nancy Padak, Ed.D., is an active researcher, author, and consultant. She was a Distinguished Professor in the College and Graduate School of Education, Health, and Human Services at Kent State University. She directed KSU's Reading and Writing Center and taught in the area of literacy education. She was the Principal Investigator for the Ohio Literacy Resource Center, which has provided support for adult and family literacy programs since 1993. Prior to her arrival at Kent State in 1985, she was a classroom teacher and district administrator. She has written or edited more than 25 books and more than 90 chapters and articles. She has also served in a variety of leadership roles in professional organizations, including the presidency of the College Reading Association and (with others) the Editor of *The Reading Teacher* and the *Journal of Literacy Research.* She has won several awards for her scholarship and contributions to literacy education.

About the Authors *(cont.)*

Rick M. Newton, Ph.D., holds a doctoral degree in Greek and Latin from the University of Michigan and is now an emeritus professor of Greek and Latin at Kent State University. He developed the course "English Words from Classical Elements," which more than 15,000 Kent State students have taken over the past 30 years. He holds the Distinguished Teaching Award from the Kent State College of Arts and Sciences and the Translation Award from the Modern Greek Studies Association of North America and Canada.

Evangeline Newton, Ph.D., is a professor of literacy education at the University of Akron, where she served as the first director of the Center for Literacy. She teaches a variety of literacy methods courses and professional development workshops to elementary, middle, and high school teachers. A former coeditor of *The Ohio Reading Teacher*, Evangeline currently chairs the Reading Review Board of the Ohio Resource Center for Mathematics, Science, and Reading. She serves on editorial review boards for *The Reading Teacher* and *Reading Horizons*. Evangeline is active in the Association of Literacy Educators and the International Reading Association (IRA). As a participant in IRA's Reading and Writing for Critical Thinking project, Evangeline taught workshops for teachers and Peace Corps volunteers in Armenia. A former St. Louis public school teacher, Evangeline holds a B.A. from Washington University in St. Louis, an M.A.T. from Webster University, and a Ph.D. from Kent State University.

Two-Syllable Compound Words

Standards: Uses word origins and derivations to understand word meaning (McREL 2.0)
Uses a variety of sentence structures to expand and embed ideas (McREL 2.3)
Uses conventions of spelling in written compositions (McREL 3.9)
Uses basic elements of structural analysis to decode unknown words (McREL 4.0)
Draws conclusions and makes inferences based on explicit and implicit information in texts (McREL 7.5)

Materials

- *Divide and Conquer: Two-Syllable Compound Words* (page 26)

- *Combine and Create: Two-Syllable Compound Words* (page 27)

- *Read and Reason: Two-Syllable Compound Words* (pages 28–30)

Teaching Tips

- A compound word contains two or more complete words joined together to create a new word. Since each word within a compound word has a meaning by itself, compound words are a good way to introduce the critical concept that word parts can have meaning as well as sound. For example, the two words *pop* and *corn* combine to form the compound word *popcorn* (i.e., "corn" that "pops" when heated).

- The second word in a compound word usually describes the main idea. The first word gives a detail about the main idea: a *birthday* is the "day of your birth."

Guided Practice

Activate Background Knowledge

1. Review the concept of compound words by asking students to give examples. Then, ask someone to explain what a compound word is (a single word that contains two or more complete words).

2. Tell students that words are often made up of recognizable parts that can help them unlock the meaning of unfamiliar words. When we identify the parts within a word, we "divide and conquer" it.

3. Write several compound words on the board (e.g., *birthday, toothbrush, mailbox, skateboard*). Ask students to choose one compound, tell what two words it contains, and tell what it means. As students offer explanations, reinforce that the meaning of a compound word is built from the semantic relationship between the two units: a *skateboard* is a "board" you "skate" on.

Divide and Conquer

4. Tell students that they have just used a strategy called Divide and Conquer that can be used to figure out the meaning of many words. Tell them that when they meet an unknown word, they can try to figure it out by "dividing and conquering" it.

5. Distribute copies of the *Divide and Conquer: Two-Syllable Compound Words* activity sheet (page 26) to students. Guide them through the activity. As each word is completed, ask a student to explain its meaning.

Two-Syllable Compound Words *(cont.)*

Guided Practice *(cont.)* ··············

Combine and Create

6. Distribute copies of the *Combine and Create: Two-Syllable Compound Words* activity sheet (page 27) to students. Tell students they will work in pairs to generate new compound words. Using and hearing new words is an important part of learning them, so invite students to share their words and sentences.

Read and Reason

7. Distribute copies of the *Read and Reason: Two-Syllable Compound Words* activity sheets (pages 28–30) to students. Have them read one or both passages and answer the comprehension questions. If the passages are too difficult for independent reading, ask students to read in pairs or follow along as you read aloud. If you choose to read aloud, tell students to raise their hands when they hear a compound word. Circle the words they identify. Then, discuss the passage. Return to each of the words you have circled and ask volunteers to explain what they mean. Then, invite students to answer the questions.

:···
: **Extend and Explore**
: Choose from among the
: activities located on the
: Teacher Resource CD to give
: students extra practice with
: compound words.
:···

Answer Key ·························

Divide and Conquer: Two-Syllable Compound Words (page 26)

Student answers for the "compound word means" section may vary.

1. birthday; birth; day; day of your birth
2. eyelid; eye; lid; lid over your eye
3. cookbook; cook; book; book with recipes
4. goldfish; gold; fish; a gold-colored fish
5. popcorn; pop; corn; corn that pops
6. weekend; week; end; the end of the week
7. beehive; bee; hive; a hive for/made by bees
8. raincoat; rain; coat; a coat for the rain

Combine and Create: Two-Syllable Compound Words (page 27)

Possible compound words may include the following:

book: *bookcase, bookends, bookmark, bookmobile, cookbook, notebook, bookshelf, bookworm, storybook, scrapbook, workbook, yearbook*

snow: *snowman, snowfall, snowflake, snowmobile, snowplow, snowsuit, snowboots, snowshoes, snowcone, snowgloves, snowstorm*

Riddle answers: *snowsuit* and *storybook*

Read and Reason: Two-Syllable Compound Words (pages 28–30)

Passage A: *birthday, weekend, snowstorm, snowsuits, snowman, mailbox, mailman, football, snowball, fireplace*

1. Answers will vary.
2. Answers will vary.
3. Answers will vary. See list above.

Passage B: *football, kneepads, headgear, sweatshirts, whichever, goaltenders, goalposts, crossbars, handbook, sometime, ballgame, fulltime, handball, whatever*

1. Answers will vary.
2. Answers will vary.
3. Answers will vary. See list above.

Name: _____   Date: _____

Divide and Conquer:
Two-Syllable Compound Words

Directions: Break apart each compound word below and write a simple definition for each word. An example has been done for you.

compound word	base word	base word	compound word means
❶ birthday	birth	day	day of your birth
❷ eyelid			
❸ cookbook			
❹ goldfish			
❺ popcorn			
❻ weekend			
❼ beehive			
❽ raincoat			

Name: _____ Date: _____

Combine and Create:
Two-Syllable Compound Words

Directions: Work with a partner to fill in the blanks with as many compound words as you can that use each of these words.

compound words with the word *book*	compound words with the word *snow*

Helpful hints to create compound words:

Compound words with the word *book*:

- What do you use to mark your place in a book?
- What do you call the heavy things that you place at the two ends of a row of books?
- What do you call a book that you use to record your notes?
- What do you call a book in which you collect scraps?

Compound words with the word *snow*:

- What do you call a heavy storm of snow?
- What kind of creature is "Frosty" in the winter song?
- What do you call a flake of snow?

. . . .

Directions: Read the riddles below. One riddle has a compound word from *book*, and the other riddle has a compound word from *snow*.

I am clothing.

My job is to keep you warm.

You will see me on the playground.

I am a _____.

I tell stories.

You can read me.

I can make you laugh or cry.

I am a _____.

On a separate sheet of paper, make up two riddles of your own using compound words. Then, trade riddles with a friend. Try to figure out each other's riddles.

Name: _____   Date: _____

Read and Reason:
Two-Syllable Compound Words

Directions: Read the passages. Circle the compound words. Then, answer the questions on page 30.

Passage A

Dear Diary,

It was my birthday last weekend. It started snowing on Wednesday. By the time the weekend came, the snowstorm had closed many roads. I had to cancel my birthday party because of the weather. I was sad until my parents had a great idea. They said the weather would help me have a wonderful birthday. And it did! Here is what happened.

First, we all put our snowsuits on. We wore mittens and hats and boots, too. Then we walked to the mailbox to see if I had any birthday cards. I did, and the mailman also brought me a present. When I opened the box, I saw a new football from my uncle. How perfect! My family played snow football. Everyone slipped and fell and laughed. We had so much fun.

Then we had Snow Olympics. There were three events. First, we each made a snow angel. Then we had a snowball fight. Finally we made a snow family. Our family had a snowman, a snow woman, two snow children, and a snow cat!

We were wet and tired after all that play in the snow. My mom built a fire in our fireplace, and my dad made us hot chocolate. Then everyone sang "Happy Birthday to You." My family and I had so much fun. Not even a snowstorm could ruin a perfect birthday!

Read and Reason:
Two-Syllable Compound Words *(cont.)*

Passage B

Let's Play Football!

Although we may think of football as a particular game, the term actually refers to a number of team sports. In the United States, we think of football as one game. It can be played by professional athletes wearing kneepads and headgear or by amateurs wearing sweatshirts. But in other parts of the world, *football* is what we in the United States call *soccer*. Unqualified, the word *football* applies to whichever form of the game is the most popular in the regional context in which the word appears.

All forms of football share some characteristics. For example, all are team sports that involve kicking a ball with the foot in order to score a goal. In American football, points can also be scored by running over the goal line or by catching a ball in the goal area. In all forms of football, defensive teams attempt to prevent scoring. Some forms have goaltenders to prevent scoring, while others have goalposts with crossbars. All forms have clearly defined playing areas, and players who go offside are penalized.

Since ancient times, people have played games that involve kicking or carrying a ball. The ancient Greeks and Romans played ball games, some of which involved the use of the feet. A Chinese military handbook, dating sometime between the third and first century B.C., describes a ballgame resembling football. Most modern forms of football have their origins in Western Europe, especially England.

Certain aspects of football have always been controversial. Today's controversies surround, among other things, workouts in hot conditions and the use of performance-enhancing drugs by full-time athletes. Controversies from long ago focused on play versus work and even betting! In 1363, King Edward III of England issued a proclamation banning "…handball, football, or hockey… or other such idle games." This shows that "football"—whatever its exact form at the time—was different from games involving other parts of the body, such as handball. And in 1409, King Henry IV forbade the "levying of money for foteball." Football, whatever its specific meaning, has a long and rich history.

Read and Reason: Two-Syllable Compound Words *(cont.)*

Directions: Read Passage A and respond to the questions below.

❶ Which snowy birthday activity is your favorite? Why?

_____

_____

❷ What would you do if you were trapped in the house by lots of snow or rain?

_____

_____

_____

❸ Pick out five compound words from Passage A and write them out:

First Word +	Second Word =	Compound Word

· ·

Directions: Read Passage B and respond to the questions below.

❶ Why do you think football has such a long history?

_____

_____

❷ What do you think is the most important similarity among various forms of football? Why?

_____

_____

_____

❸ Find five different compound words from Passage B. Write them out here.

First Word +	Second Word =	Compound Word

Three-Syllable Compound Words

Standards: Uses word origins and derivations to understand word meaning (McREL 2.0)
Uses a variety of sentence structures to expand and embed ideas (McREL 2.3)
Uses conventions of spelling in written compositions (McREL 3.9)
Uses basic elements of structural analysis to decode unknown words (McREL 4.0)
Draws conclusions and makes inferences based on explicit and implicit information in texts (McREL 7.5)

Materials

- *Divide and Conquer: Three-Syllable Compound Words* (page 34)

- *Combine and Create: Three-Syllable Compound Words* (page 35)

- *Read and Reason: Three-Syllable Compound Words* (pages 36–38)

Teaching Tips

- **Reminder:** A compound word contains two or more *word units* joined together to create a new word. Since each unit within a compound has a meaning by itself, compound words are a good way to introduce the critical concept that word parts can have *meaning* as well as sound.

- Because three-syllable compound words contain only two semantic units, remind students to look for meaning over sound relationships when dividing and conquering new words. *Fingernail,* for example, has three sound units (*fing/ er/nail*) but only two meaning units (*finger/nail*).

Teaching Tips *(cont.)*

- By examining compound words of three syllables, students learn to divide a word correctly into its component parts that make sense on their own. For example, in the word *Spiderman,* students will readily identify the component parts as *spider* and *man,* not as *spi-* and *-derman.* This is because, when we look at a word, we look for meaningful parts that it contains (i.e., we do not only look for units of sound).

- Remind students that the second word in a compound word usually describes the main idea. The first word gives a detail about the main idea*: A firefighter* is someone who "fights" "fires." A *fingernail* is a "nail" on the "finger."

Guided Practice

Activating Background Knowledge

1. Review the concept of compound words by asking students to explain what a compound word is (a single word that contains two or more complete words).

2. Write a few two-syllable compound words in one column (e.g., *eyelid, beehive, mailbox*) and a few three-syllable words in a second column (e.g., *honeybee, loudspeaker, waterfall*). Ask volunteers to "divide and conquer" by selecting a word and telling what two words it contains. As students offer explanations, reinforce that the meaning of each compound word is built from the semantic (i.e., the meaning-based) relationship between the two units (an *eyelid* is a "lid" over your "eye"; a *honeybee* is a "bee" that makes "honey").

Three-Syllable Compound Words *(cont.)*

Guided Practice *(cont.)* ··············

3. After all the words have been analyzed, point out that while each column contains compound words, one column has words with two syllables and the other has words with three syllables. Point out that when we "divide" words into parts, we look for word parts that have meaning. Demonstrate by pointing out that students could not figure out the meaning of the word *waterfall* if they divided it by syllables (*wat/er/fall*) instead of meaning (*water/fall*).

Divide and Conquer

4. Distribute copies of the *Divide and Conquer: Three-Syllable Compound Words* activity sheet (page 34) to students. Guide students through the activity. You may duplicate the practice sheet for each student and/or project it on an overhead projector. As each word is completed, ask a student to explain what it means. Make sure their definitions make sense.

Combine and Create

5. Distribute copies of the *Combine and Create: Three-Syllable Compound Words* activity sheet (page 35) to students. Ask students to work in pairs and generate new compound words. Make sure students have an opportunity to share the words and sentences they have made with classmates, because using and hearing new words is an important part of learning them.

Read and Reason

6. Distribute copies of the *Read and Reason: Three-Syllable Compound Words* activity sheets (page 36–38) to students. Have students read one or both passages and answer the comprehension questions. If the passages are too difficult for independent reading, ask students to read in pairs or follow along as you read aloud. Tell them to raise their hands when they hear a compound word of two or more syllables. Circle the words they identify. After you have finished reading, discuss the passage. Return to each of the circled words and ask volunteers to explain what they mean. Then, invite students to answer the questions.

Extend and Explore
Choose from among the activities located on the Teacher Resource CD to give students extra practice with compound words.

Three-Syllable Compound Words (cont.)

Answer Key ·······················

Divide and Conquer: Three-Syllable Compound Words (page 34)

Student answers for the "compound word means" section may vary.

1. honeybee: honey; bee; a bee that makes honey
2. newspaper: news; paper; a paper filled with news
3. flowerpot: flower; pot; a pot for flowers or plants
4. tablespoon: table; spoon; a spoon that is used for serving at the table
5. sunglasses: sun; glasses; glasses made to protect your eyes from the sun
6. blueberry: blue; berry; a berry that is blue
7. grandmother: grand; mother; a mother who is older than the mother; the mother of my father and/or mother
8. rainwater: rain; water; water that is caused by the rain

Combine and Create: Three-Syllable Compound Words (page 35)

Possible compound words may include *supermarket, superstar, supermodel; grandfather, grandparent, granddaughter; honeybee, honeymoon, honeycomb; handwoven, handkerchief, handwriting*

Student sentences will vary.

Read and Reason: Three-Syllable Compound Words (pages 36–38)

Passage A: *grandchildren, grandparents, weekend, blueberries, grandpa, strawberry, breakfast, weatherman, thunderstorms, firefighters, roundabout, overpass, downtown, bottleneck, something, great-grandchildren*

1. Answers will vary.
2. Answers will vary.
3. Answers will vary. See list above.

Passage B: *sometimes, countertops, outdoors, thunderbolts, fingernails, dishwasher, platewarmer, mountaintops, windowsills, peppermint, peacemaker, overhead, baseboard, pullout, furthermore, overload*

1. Answers will vary.
2. Answers will vary.
3. Answers will vary. See list above.

Name: _____ Date: _____

Divide and Conquer: Three-Syllable Compound Words

Directions: Break apart each compound word below and write a simple definition for each word. An example has been done for you.

compound word	base word	base word	compound word means
❶ honeybee	honey	bee	a bee that makes honey
❷ newspaper			
❸ flowerpot			
❹ tablespoon			
❺ sunglasses			
❻ blueberry			
❼ grandmother			
❽ rainwater			

Name: _____   Date: _____

Combine and Create: Three-Syllable Compound Words

Directions: Form 12 compound words by combining the single words in the columns below. Column A lists the first unit of each compound word. Combine each single word in Column A with three single words from Column B to create compound words that make sense. Each compound word you create will have three or more syllables.

Column A (first part of the word)	Column B (second part of the word)
super	bee
grand	father
honey	market
hand	woven
	moon
	star
	model
	comb
	kerchief
	parent
	daughter
	writing

My compound words are:

super: _____

grand: _____

honey: _____

hand: _____

Now, use your favorite compound word from the above list in a short sentence:

_____

_____

_____

Name: _____   Date: _____

Read and Reason: Three-Syllable Compound Words

Directions: Read the passages. Circle the compound words containing two or more syllables. Then, answer the questions on page 38.

Passage A

Grandchildren's Weekend

My grandparents live by a lake. One weekend every summer, they invite their eleven grandchildren to "Grandchildren's Weekend" at their lake house. It's always an adventure.

One summer, we went to pick blueberries. Grandpa's rule was that we couldn't eat more than we put in our baskets. The blueberries were so plump and juicy that it was hard to follow Grandpa's rule. We all had blue tongues and lips by the time we went home. If Grandpa had had a strawberry patch, we would have turned our tongues red!

The next day, we made blueberry jam and blueberry pies. We had the jam on toast for breakfast. We had blueberry pie for dessert.

Last summer was a little scary. The weatherman predicted thunderstorms. His prediction was correct! The sky turned gray-green, and the wind howled. We could see the storm coming down the lake. We lost electricity, but we were safe in the house. After the storm was over, we heard sirens and saw firefighters rushing roundabout. The storm had knocked down telephone poles and were blocking the overpass that led to downtown. The traffic in that area was a bottleneck.

Every summer brings something new at "Grandchildren's Weekend." We all look forward to each visit. We have told Grandmother and Grandfather that when we have our own children, we hope they will have "Great-grandchildren's Weekends" for them.

Read and Reason: Three-Syllable Compound Words *(cont.)*

Passage B

Dear Diary,

Sometimes I just shake my head at my parents. They find the silliest things to argue about! They have been arguing for the past several weeks about how to remodel our kitchen. They have been having the "Kitchen Battles."

Take countertops, for example. You would think they would be easy to select, but no! My dad prefers colors related to the outdoors, so he wants lines of color on the countertops that look like thunderbolts. My mom is concerned about hygiene, so she scrapes her fingernails over each sample to see if it is porous. So far, they have not selected a countertop that meets both their criteria, and my mom's fingernails are a mess!

Appliances are also a bone of contention. Who knew there were so many choices? The other day I heard them trying to select a dishwasher. You would think color and capacity would be the issues, and they were. But they also had to consider price, energy efficiency, environmental impact, and even level of sanitizing. My mom decided she wanted a dishwasher that had a plate-warmer button!

Even windows have caused lengthy conversations. Since the kitchen will be completely gutted, we can decide where the new windows will be. My dad wants a western view because he likes to look at the mountaintops in the distance. My mom wants a southern view because she likes to grow herbs on the windowsills. She says the western sun will burn her herbs and peppermint plants. Trying to be the peacemaker, I suggested windows in both directions, but they both just scowled at me. I'm staying out of it!

Nothing is easy with this kitchen! Decisions must be made about overhead cabinets, baseboard trim, and pullout shelving. Furthermore, with so many appliances, we need to take care not to overload our electrical circuits! We are all looking forward to the completion of this project. Not only will we have a lovely new room, but my parents will no longer have all these decisions to argue about.

Read and Reason: Three-Syllable
Compound Words *(cont.)*

Directions: Read Passage A and respond to the questions below.

❶ How do you think the grandparents decide what to do with their grandchildren?

_____

_____

❷ Write about something your family likes to do together.

_____

_____

❸ Find three compound words from Passage A and write them out here:

First Word +	Second Word =	Compound Word

· ·

Directions: Read Passage B and respond to the questions below.

❶ Do the disagreements make sense to you? Why?

_____

_____

❷ How do you think these disagreements should be resolved? Why?

_____

_____

❸ Find three compound words from Passage B and write them out here:

First Word +	Second Word =	Compound Word

Negative Prefix *un-*

Standards: Uses word origins and derivations to understand word meaning (McREL 2.0)
Uses a variety of sentence structures to expand and embed ideas (McREL 2.3)
Uses conventions of spelling in written compositions (McREL 3.9)
Uses basic elements of structural analysis to decode unknown words (McREL 4.0)
Draws conclusions and makes inferences based on explicit and implicit information in texts (McREL 7.5)

Materials

- *Divide and Conquer: Negative Prefix un-* (page 41)
- *Combine and Create: Negative Prefix un-* (page 42)
- *Read and Reason: Negative Prefix un-* (pages 43–45)

Teaching Tips

- Prefixes affect the meaning of a word by negating it, providing direction, or adding emphasis.

- The most common prefix in English is *un-* (not). It negates a word.

- The base, not the prefix, provides a word's main meaning. Some prefixes attach to whole words as well as bases. The prefix *un-* frequently attaches to whole words.

Guided Practice

Activate Background Knowledge

1. Review the concept of a *prefix* (unit added to the front of a word that influences its meaning). Tell students that *un-* is a prefix meaning "not." Write the words *able, tie,* and *happy* on the board. Explain that each of these words can be negated with the prefix *un-*. Then, add *un-* to the front of each word.

2. Working with partners or in whole-class discussion, ask students to tell what each of the words means. Then, ask them to explain how the prefix changes the meaning of the word. For example, the word *unable* = "not" "able" to do something. The prefix *un-* negates the original word ("unable" from "able").

3. Invite students to brainstorm more *un-* words. Ask them to pick a word from the list, tell what it means, and explain how adding the *un-* prefix changes the meaning.

Divide and Conquer

4. Distribute copies of the *Divide and Conquer: Negative Prefix un-* activity sheet (page 41) to students. Guide students through the activity. The practice sheet may be duplicated for each student and/or projected on a projector. As each word is completed, ask a student to explain what it means. Make sure the definitions make sense. In this exercise, students are to translate the prefix *un-* as "not."

Negative Prefix *un-* (cont.)

Guided Practice (cont.) · · · · · · · · · · · ·

Combine and Create

5. Distribute copies of the *Combine and Create: Negative Prefix un-* activity sheet (page 42). Have students work in pairs to generate new words with the *un-* prefix. Encourage students to share the words and sentences they have made with classmates. Using and hearing new words is an important part of learning them.

Read and Reason

6. Distribute copies of the *Read and Reason: Negative Prefix un-* activity sheets (pages 43–45) to students. Have students read one or both passages and answer the comprehension questions. The passages include words beginning with the negating prefix *un-*. If the passages are too difficult for independent reading, ask students to read in pairs or follow along as you read aloud. Tell them to raise their hands when they hear a word with the prefix *un-*. Circle the words they identify. After you have finished reading, discuss the passage. Return to each of the circled words and ask volunteers to explain what they mean. Then, invite students to answer the questions.

> **Extend and Explore**
> Choose from among the activities located on the Teacher Resource CD to give students extra practice with *un-* words.

Answer Key ·

Divide and Conquer: Negative Prefix *un-* (page 41)

1. unsafe: not; safe; not safe
2. unwell: not; well ; not well
3. unclean: not; clean; not clean
4. unexpected: not; expected; not expected
5. unzipped: not; zipped; not zipped
6. unpacked: not; packed; not packed
7. unbelievable: not; believable; not believable
8. unlucky: not; lucky; not lucky

Combine and Create: Negative Prefix *un-* (page 42)

Students' answers will vary. Possible answers include:

1. I am unsure.
2. It is untidy.
3. I am uncertain.
4. It was unbreakable.
5. It was unwanted.
6. They were unkind.
7. They are uneven.

Synonym *un-* words will vary. In this list, the two synonym words are *unsure* and *uncertain*.

Read and Reason: Negative Prefix *un-* (pages 43–45)

Passage A: *unable, unhappy, unlucky, unclean, uncross*

1. Answers will vary.
2. Answers will vary.
3. Answers will vary. See list above.

Passage B: *unforgettable, unsatisfied, unchallenged, untapped, unbroken, unable, unbounded, unequalled, unfortunately, unwilling, uncommon, unbigoted, uninterrupted*

1. Answers will vary.
2. Answers will vary.
3. Answers will vary. See list above.

Name: _____   Date: _____

Divide and Conquer: Negative Prefix *un-*

Directions: Break apart each word below. Write the prefix and its meaning, the base word, and a simple definition for each word. An example has been done for you.

word	prefix means	base word	definition
❶ unsafe	un- = not	safe	not safe
❷ unwell			
❸ unclean			
❹ unexpected			
❺ unzipped			
❻ unpacked			
❼ unbelievable			
❽ unlucky			

Name: _____   Date: _____

Combine and Create: Negative Prefix _un-_

Directions: Work with a partner. Create a word beginning with the prefix _un-_ that best describes the situations below.

The situation is...	The _un-_ word is...
❶ I am not sure of myself.	I am _____.
❷ My room is not tidy.	It is _____.
❸ I am not certain about my answer.	I am _____.
❹ The athlete's record could not be broken.	It was _____.
❺ Nobody wanted that stray dog.	It was _____.
❻ Your remarks were not kind.	They were _____.
❼ One and three are not even numbers.	They are _____.

Of the 7 _un-_ words you have written, which two are synonyms (have the same meaning)?

_____ and _____

Name: _____   Date: _____

Read and Reason: Negative Prefix _un-_

Directions: Read the passages. Circle the words with the prefix _un-_. Then, answer the questions on page 45.

Passage A

Are You Able or Unable?

Unable? Maybe not. Give it a try! You may be more able than you think.

Are you unhappy? Find something to laugh about. Then you will not be unhappy. You will be happy.

Are you unlucky? Look for a four-leaf clover. Some people think four-leaf clovers bring good luck.

Are you unclean? That's an easy one—take a bath!

Are you able to cross your arms? To uncross them?

See? You are more able than you think. You are not unable!

Read and Reason: Negative Prefix *un-* (cont.)

Passage B

Unforgettable

Nat King Cole was an American pianist, singer, and bandleader. He was born in Alabama in 1917. His musical career began at age 12 when he started playing the piano and organ in his father's church. He was unsatisfied with this career, however. He felt unchallenged by church music, since it left his greater musical skills untapped. In the late 1930s and 1940s, he assembled several jazz groups that gave concerts and made records.

Cole found his greatest success when he began performing as a solo singer. He had several hit records in the 1940s and 1950s. Noted for his warm tone and smooth, unbroken phrasing, Cole was regarded as one of the top male vocalists in the United States. Some jazz critics regretted that he was unable to play piano himself while making these recordings. Other critics found his sincere, husky voice and unbounded enthusiasm on stage unequalled among his peers.

Cole was the first African American to host a network television program, *The Nat King Cole Show*, which debuted in 1956. Unfortunately, the show fell victim to the bigotry of the times. It was canceled after one season because most sponsors were unwilling to be associated with a black entertainer. Outspoken racial prejudice was not uncommon at the time.

Concert audiences were unbigoted, however. Cole enjoyed uninterrupted success on stage until his death in 1965. His musical style shifted toward mainstream pop. Many music historians believe that the prejudices of the era hindered Cole's potential for even greater stardom. Nat King Cole's songs are still played today. In fact, his daughter Natalie, also a singer, achieved her greatest musical success in 1991 with "Unforgettable," an electronically created duet with her father.

Read and Reason: Negative Prefix *un-* (cont.)

Directions: Read Passage A and respond to the questions below.

❶ Name something that you were once unable to do but can now do. How did you learn to do this thing?

_____

_____

_____

❷ Name something that you are unable to do but wish to learn to do. How will you learn to do this thing?

_____

_____

_____

❸ Pick four words from Passage A that have the prefix *un-*.

words with the prefix *un-*
_____   _____
_____   _____

Directions: Read Passage B and respond to the questions below.

❶ Why do you think sponsors were unwilling to air commercials on Cole's TV program?

_____

_____

❷ Why do you think audiences attended his concerts, despite the bigotry of the times?

_____

_____

❸ Write six words from Passage B that have the prefix *un-*.

words with the prefix *un-*
_____   _____
_____   _____
_____   _____

Negative Prefix *in-*

Standards: Uses word origins and derivations to understand word meaning (McREL 2.0)

Uses a variety of sentence structures to expand and embed ideas (McREL 2.3)

Uses conventions of spelling in written compositions (McREL 3.9)

Uses basic elements of structural analysis to decode unknown words (McREL 4.0)

Draws conclusions and makes inferences based on explicit and implicit information in texts (McREL 7.5)

Materials

- *Divide and Conquer: Negative Prefix in-* (page 49)
- *Combine and Create: Negative Prefix in-* (page 50)
- *Read and Reason: Negative Prefix in-* (pages 51–53)

Teaching Tips

- The English language has two prefixes (*in-*) spelled alike. This lesson focuses on negative *in-*. The prefix *in-* means "not" in words like *inhuman* (cruel and "not" human) and *inflexible* ("not" flexible).

- The other prefix *in-* is directional, meaning "in, on, into." It appears in words like *induct* (to lead "into" the army; to lead "into" the hall of fame) and *inhabit* (to live "in" an area). If you want to teach these two prefixes in sequence, follow this lesson with Lesson 11 (page 104).

- It is not difficult to distinguish between negative *in-* and directional *in-*. Words starting with negative *in-* usually have a negative meaning.

Teaching Tips *(cont.)*

- The prefix *in-* can undergo assimilation (page 6) and appear as *im-* and *il-*. The assimilated forms *im-* and *il-* are presented in Lesson 5 (page 54).

- The negating prefix *in-* attaches to both whole words and Latin bases. For example, the adjective *incapable* is the negative of the positive word *capable*, but the word *intact*, meaning "whole, not broken," begins with the negating prefix *in-*, and attaches to a Latin base *tact-*, which means "touched." Something "intact" is whole and unbroken because it is, literally, "not" (*in-*) "touched." The words presented in this lesson attach the prefix *in-* to whole words.

Guided Practice

Activate Background Knowledge

1. Review the concept of a *prefix* (unit added to the front of a word that influences its meaning). Explain that *in-* is a negating prefix meaning "not." Write the words *correct* and *visible* on the board. Point out that each of these words can be negated with the prefix *in-*. Then, add *in-* to each word.

2. Working with partners or in whole-class discussion, ask students to tell what each word means. Then, ask them to explain how the prefix changes the meaning (*incorrect* means "not" "correct"). Adding the prefix *in-* negates the original word.

Negative Prefix *in-* *(cont.)*

Guided Practice *(cont.)* ·············

3. Write the word *incredible* on the board. Now put a slash between *in* and *credible* (*in/credible*). Tell students that *cred* is a Latin base that means "believe." Point out that something incredible is "not" "believable." Ask a few students to think of something we might consider "incredible" (e.g., snow in the summer, flying saucers). Ask students to share examples of what they consider incredible.

4. Invite students to brainstorm more negative *in-* words. Ask them to pick a word from the list, tell what it means, and explain how adding the prefix *in-* negates the meaning.

Divide and Conquer

5. Distribute copies of the *Divide and Conquer: Negative Prefix in-* activity sheet (page 49) to students. Guide them through the activity. The sheet may be duplicated for each student and/or projected on a projector. As each word is completed, ask a student to select the best answer from the Answer Bank and to explain why he or she chose the definition. Make sure students use "not" in their oral answers.

Combine and Create

6. Distribute copies of the *Combine and Create: Negative Prefix in-* activity sheet (page 50) to students. Ask students to work in pairs to generate new words. Make sure students have an opportunity to share the words and sentences they have made with classmates because using and hearing new words is an important part of learning them.

Read and Reason

7. Distribute copies of the *Read and Reason: Negative Prefix in-* activity sheets (pages 51–53) to students. Have students read one or both passages and answer the comprehension questions. If the passages are too difficult for independent reading, ask them to read in pairs or follow along as you read aloud. Tell them to raise their hands when they hear a word which contains the negating prefix. Circle the words they identify. After you have finished reading, discuss the passage. Return to each of the words you have circled and ask volunteers to explain what they mean. Then, invite students to answer the questions.

> **Extend and Explore**
> Choose from among the activities located on the Teacher Resource CD to give students extra practice with negative *in-* words.

Answer Key ·····················

Divide and Conquer: Negative Prefix *in-* (page 49)

1. insensitive: not; sensitive; I
2. independent: not; dependent; H
3. indescribable: not; describable; G
4. inflexible: not; flexible; D
5. inedible: not; edible; E
6. inoperable: not; operable; F
7. inanimate: not; animate; C
8. inaccurate: not; accurate; B
9. incomplete: not; complete; J
10. inexpensive: not; expensive; A

Negative Prefix *in-* (cont.)

Answer Key (cont.) ·················

Combine and Create: Negative Prefix *in-*
(page 50)

in- means "not": *incorrect, inactive, incapable, insane, inflexible* (*Note:* these words have a clearly negative meaning, a sign of negative *in-*.)

in- does not mean "not": *inhale, income, inspire, inhabit, inject* (*Note:* these words begin with directional *in-*.)

Students' sentences will vary.

Read and Reason: Negative Prefix *in-*
(pages 51–53)

Passage A: *inedible, indigestible, inactive, indifferent, incurable, inoperable*

1. A dog or cat that vomits many times may be sick from eating something either inedible or indigestible. A normally lively and energetic animal that suddently becomes inactive may be sick. A pet that stops eating or drinking may also be sick.

2. Answers will vary.

3. *inactive*; also accept *indifferent*

Passage B: *incredible, inhuman, involuntarily, injustice, invincible, indefatigable, inactivity, incongruous, inexplicable, incessantly*

1. Answers will vary.

2. Answers will vary.

3. *Invincible* means incapable of being conquered. Students should explain what the word means and use the word *not* within their explanations.

Name: _____ Date: _____

Divide and Conquer: Negative Prefix *in-*

Directions: Break apart each word below. Write the prefix, its meaning, what the base word is, and select a definition from the Answer Bank below. An example has been done for you.

Answer Bank
A. cheap or low-priced
B. wrong or mistaken
C. not lively, not moving; not endowed with breath or life
D. rigid and unbending
E. not fit for consumption
F. not suitable for surgery
G. surpassing description
H. self-governing; not reliant on others for support
I. lacking feeling; not sensitive to others
J. not finished

word	prefix means	base word	definition
❶ insensitive	in- = not	sensitive	I
❷ independent			
❸ indescribable			
❹ inflexible			
❺ inedible			
❻ inoperable			
❼ inanimate			
❽ inaccurate			
❾ incomplete			
❿ inexpensive			

Name: _____ Date: _____

Combine and Create: Negative Prefix _in-_

Directions: Sometimes _in-_ means "not," but sometimes it does not. Five of the words in the Word Bank begin with the prefix _in-_ and mean "not," and the other five do not. Which of these words means "not," and which do not? Sort the words in the correct columns. _Hint:_ Which of these words has a negative meaning?

Word Bank				
incorrect	inactive	inhale	income	inspire
inhabit	inflexible	inject	incapable	insane

_in-_ means "not"   _in-_ does not mean "not"

❶ _____   ❻ _____

❷ _____   ❼ _____

❸ _____   ❽ _____

❹ _____   ❾ _____

❺ _____   ❿ _____

Directions: Write two sentences using two words with in- that mean "not".

_____

_____

_____

_____

_____

_____

Name: _____   Date: _____

Read and Reason: Negative Prefix *in-*

Directions: Read the passages. Circle the words with the prefix *in-*. Then, answer the questions on page 53.

Passage A

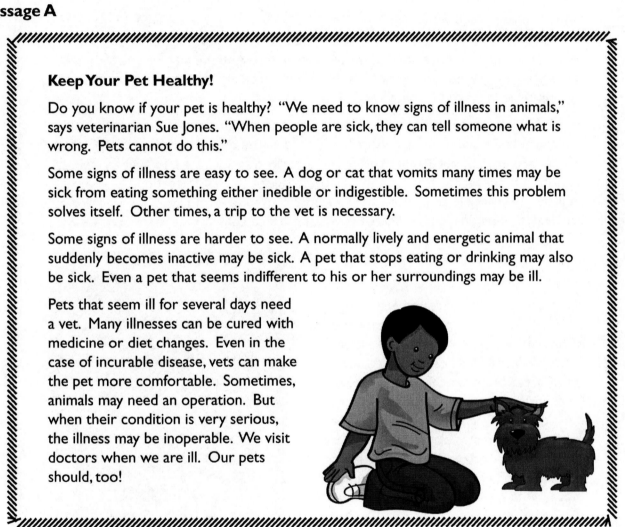

Keep Your Pet Healthy!

Do you know if your pet is healthy? "We need to know signs of illness in animals," says veterinarian Sue Jones. "When people are sick, they can tell someone what is wrong. Pets cannot do this."

Some signs of illness are easy to see. A dog or cat that vomits many times may be sick from eating something either inedible or indigestible. Sometimes this problem solves itself. Other times, a trip to the vet is necessary.

Some signs of illness are harder to see. A normally lively and energetic animal that suddenly becomes inactive may be sick. A pet that stops eating or drinking may also be sick. Even a pet that seems indifferent to his or her surroundings may be ill.

Pets that seem ill for several days need a vet. Many illnesses can be cured with medicine or diet changes. Even in the case of incurable disease, vets can make the pet more comfortable. Sometimes, animals may need an operation. But when their condition is very serious, the illness may be inoperable. We visit doctors when we are ill. Our pets should, too!

Read and Reason: Negative Prefix _in-_ (cont.)

Passage B

The Incredible Hulk

What happens when you get angry? Can you feel your heart pounding? Does your breath quicken? If you were the Incredible Hulk, all this would happen and more. You would grow huge muscles, and you would turn green. And the angrier you became, the bigger and greener you would become. The Incredible Hulk is a character that has appeared in Marvel Comics since 1962.

The Incredible Hulk is the inhuman alter ego of the withdrawn and reserved scientist Dr. Bruce Banner, who was accidentally exposed to the detonation of a bomb he had created. After the blast, Banner began involuntarily transforming into a giant, raging, humanoid monster. Both anger and injustice trigger this transformation. As the Hulk, he is nearly invincible and certainly indefatigable. Eventually, though, after a period of inactivity, the Incredible Hulk settles down, and Bruce Banner reappears. Since the personalities of the man and the monster are incongruous, Banner's life is complicated and sometimes inexplicable.

The Incredible Hulk's creator, Stan Lee, says the character was inspired by a combination of _Dr. Jekyll and Mr. Hyde_ and _Frankenstein_. From Jekyll and Hyde came the idea for transformation. As to the influence of Frankenstein, Lee said, "I had always loved the old movie _Frankenstein_. And it seemed to me that the monster, played by Boris Karloff, wasn't really a bad guy. He was the good guy. He didn't want to hurt anybody. It's just those idiots with torches kept running up and down the mountains incessantly, chasing him and getting him angry."

Read and Reason: Negative Prefix *in-* (cont.)

Directions: Read Passage A and respond to the questions below.

❶ How can you tell if a pet is sick?

_____

_____

_____

❷ Compare pet symptoms to human symptoms. How are they alike?

_____

_____

_____

❸ In the passage, what word is the antonym (has the opposite meaning) of lively and energetic?

_____

Directions: Read Passage B and respond to the questions below.

❶ How could the Incredible Hulk's physical transformation be symbolic?

_____

_____

_____

❷ Why do you think comicbook lovers are drawn to superheroes?

_____

_____

_____

❸ Can you explain what the word *invincible* means? Be sure to use the word *not* in your explanation.

_____

_____

_____

_____

_____

Negative Prefixes *im-* and *il-*

Standards: Uses word origins and derivations to understand word meaning (McREL 2.0)
Uses a variety of sentence structures to expand and embed ideas (McREL 2.3)
Uses conventions of spelling in written compositions (McREL 3.9)
Uses basic elements of structural analysis to decode unknown words (McREL 4.0)
Draws conclusions and makes inferences based on explicit and implicit information in texts (McREL 7.5)

Materials

- *Divide and Conquer: Negative Prefixes im- and il-* (page 57)

- *Combine and Create: Negative Prefixes im- and il-* (page 58)

- *Read and Reason: Negative Prefixes im- and il-* (pages 59–61)

Teaching Tips

- The negative prefixes *im-* and *il-* are assimilated forms of the prefix *in-*, which was presented in the previous lesson. Negative *im-* and *il-* negate words (e.g., *impossible*, meaning "not" possible; *illegal*, meaning "not" legal).

- *Reminder:* Like the prefix *in-*, the assimilated prefixes *im-* and *il-* may also be directional, meaning "in, on, into" (e.g., *import*, meaning to "carry" "into" an area; *illuminate*, meaning to shed light "on" something). Directional *in-*, *im-*, and *il-* are presented in Unit III, Lesson 11 (page 104). If you want to teach these prefixes in sequence, follow this lesson with Lesson 11.

Teaching Tips *(cont.)*

- **Assimilation:** When a prefix attaches to a base beginning with certain consonants, it may undergo a spelling change to make the word easier to pronounce. The prefixes *im-* and *il-* are assimilated forms of the original prefix *in-*.

- **Important spelling note for Divide and Conquer:** The prefix *il-* is usually followed by a base beginning with the consonant *l*. The result is a double *ll* near the beginning of the word (e.g., *illogical, illiterate*). When students encounter words beginning with *ill-*, they should divide between the double *l* to separate the prefix from the base.

- The prefix *im-* is usually followed by a base beginning with *m* or *p* (e.g., *immodest*, meaning "not modest"; *impatient*, meaning "not patient"). Students should divide after the first *m* to separate the prefix from the base.

Guided Practice

Activate Background Knowledge

1. Write the words *impossible* and *illegible* on the board. Put a slash after *im-* and *il-*. Tell students that *im-* and *il-* are prefixes that mean "not." Write *legal* and *perfect* on the board. As they work with partners or in whole-class discussion, ask students how they would negate these words (*illegal, imperfect*). Then, ask them to explain how the prefix changes the meaning. Adding *im-* or *il-* negates the original word.

Negative Prefixes *im-* and *il-* (cont.)

Guided Practice (cont.) . . . .

2. Tell students that *im-* and *il-* are variations of the prefix *in-*. Ask them to say *impossible* and then to say *inpossible.* Which is easier to pronounce? Ask them to say *illegible* and then *inlegible.* Again, which is easier to pronounce? Explain that sometimes prefixes undergo a spelling change to simplify pronunciations. This process is called *assimilation.*

Divide and Conquer

3. Distribute copies of the *Divide and Conquer: Negative Prefixes im-* and *il-* activity sheet (page 57) to students. Guide students through the activity. The practice sheet may be duplicated for each student and/or projected on a projector. Explain that in words beginning with negative *im-*, the prefix will be followed by either the letter *p* or the letter *m*; in words beginning with *il-*, the prefix will be followed by a second *l.* As each word is completed, ask a student to select the best answer from the Answer Bank and to explain why he or she chose the definition. Make sure students use "not" in their oral answers.

Combine and Create

4. Distribute copies of the *Combine and Create: Negative Prefixes im-* and *il-* activity sheet (page 58) to students. Ask students to work in pairs to generate new negating words using *il-* and *im-*. Encourage students to share the words and sentences they have created. Using and hearing new words is an important part of learning them.

Read and Reason

5. Distribute copies of the *Read and Reason: Negative Prefixes im-* and *il-* activity sheets (pages 59–61) to students. Have students read one or both passages and answer the comprehension questions. Explain that the passages include words beginning with the negating prefixes *il-, im-,* and *in-.* If the passages are too difficult for independent reading, ask students to read in pairs or follow along as you read aloud. Tell them to raise their hands when they hear a word that contains the negating prefix *in-, im-,* or *il.* Circle the words they identify. After you have finished reading, discuss the passage. Return to each of the circled words and ask volunteers to explain what they mean. Then, invite students to answer the questions.

> **Extend and Explore**
> Choose from among the activities located on the Teacher Resource CD to give students extra practice with *im-* and *il-* words.

Negative Prefixes *im-* and *il-* (cont.)

Answer Key ·······················

Divide and Conquer: Negative Prefixes *im-* and *il-* (page 57)

1. immature: not; mature; E
2. impatient: not; patient; F
3. illegal: not; legal; H
4. immortal: not; mortal; B
5. imperfect: not; perfect; C
6. illegible: not; legible; D
7. impermanent: not; permanent; J
8. illiterate: not; literate; A
9. immeasurable: not; measurable; G
10. improper: not; proper; I

Combine and Create: Negative Prefixes *im-* and *il-* (page 58)

1. imperfect
2. improper
3. impolite
4. impossible
5. immature
6. illogical
7. illegal
8. immeasurable
9. illegible
10. illiberal

Synonyms: immature = childish

Sentences will vary.

Read and Reason: Negative Prefixes *im-* and *il-* (pages 59–61)

Passage A: *impossible, impolite, illegal, immobile*

1. Answers will vary.
2. Answers will vary.

Passage B: *immortal, impossible, improbable, illogical, incredible, immediately, immature, innumerable, imperfect, immeasurable*

1. Answers will vary.
2. Answers will vary.
3. *Improbable* and/or *illogical*

What a Negative Predicament! (page 62)

1. D
2. F
3. G
4. H
5. A
6. C
7. I
8. J
9. B
10. E

Name: _____   Date: _____

Divide and Conquer:
Negative Prefixes *im-* and *il-*

Directions: Break apart each word below. Write the prefix and its meaning, what the base word is, and select a definition from the Answer Bank below. An example has been done for you.

Answer Bank
A. unable to read or write
B. everlasting; not subject to death
C. flawed
D. unable to be read (from poor handwriting)
E. childish; not fully developed
F. short-tempered; not able to wait
G. vastly large; incapable of measurement
H. not lawful
I. indecent; not reflecting good manners or usage
J. transient, temporary

word	prefix means	base word	definition
1 immature	im- = not	mature	E
2 impatient			
3 illegal			
4 immortal			
5 imperfect			
6 illegible			
7 impermanent			
8 illiterate			
9 immeasurable			
10 improper			

Name: _____ Date: _____

Combine and Create:
Negative Prefixes *im-* and *il-*

Directions: Choose the correct prefix for each of the word definitions below. When you have finished, pick out two words you find interesting. Then, write one sentence that uses both of the words.

❶ Not perfect = _____

❷ Not proper = _____

❸ Not polite = _____

❹ Not possible = _____

❺ Not mature = _____

❻ Not logical = _____

❼ Not legal = _____

❽ Not able to be measured = _____

❾ Not legible = _____

❿ Not liberal = _____

Of the words above, which one is a synonym (means the same thing as) for the word *childish*?

_____

Choose two words from above. Write a sentence that includes both the words you chose.

_____

_____

_____

_____

_____

_____

_____

Name: _____   Date: _____

Read and Reason: Negative Prefixes *im-* and *il-*

Directions: Read the passages. Circle the words with the negative prefixes *im-* and *il-*. Then, answer the questions on page 61.

Passage A

It Depends

Is it possible or impossible to leap tall buildings in a single bound?

It depends. If you are Superman, you can. If you are not, it is impossible.

Is it polite or impolite to eat with your fingers?

It depends. If you are eating French fries, it is polite. If you are eating mashed potatoes, it is impolite.

Is it legal or illegal to be outside very late at night?

It depends. If you are an adult, it is legal. If you are a child, it may be illegal. Many towns have curfews for young people.

Is a car mobile or immobile?

It depends. If the engine is running, the car can be mobile. If the key is not in the car and the car is in park, it is immobile.

Read and Reason:
Negative Prefixes *im-* and *il-* (cont.)

Passage B

An Immortal Jellyfish?

An "immortal" jellyfish species that can age backward is invading the world's oceans, a recent study says. The tiny jellyfish, called *Turritopsis dohrnii,* is only about as large as a pinky fingernail when fully grown. It was discovered in the Mediterranean Sea in 1883, but its seemingly impossible ability was not discovered until the 1990s.

These little jellyfish usually reproduce, live, and die the old-fashioned way. Improbable and illogical as it may seem, however, something different may happen when starvation, physical damage, or other crises arise. According to study author Maria Pia Miglietta, "instead of sure death, [the jellyfish] transforms all of its existing cells." Some people find this incredible.

It immediately turns itself into a blob-like cyst, which then develops into a polyp colony. These immature cells may then be transformed. Muscle cells can become nerve cells or even sperm or eggs. Through reproduction, the new polyp colony can spawn hundreds of nearly genetically identical jellyfish. Their numbers may become innumerable and impossible to calculate. This process may be helping the jellyfish spread throughout the world's oceans.

Scientists' understanding of the immortal jellyfish is still imperfect. They do not understand the impact these tiny creatures, reproducing in immeasurable quantities, may be having on their ecosystems. Still, the creatures' very effective cellular repair mechanisms interest scientists. At the least, the discovery underscores "our remarkable underestimation of the extent to which the ocean has been reorganized," says scientist James Carlton.

Read and Reason:
Negative Prefixes *im-* and *il-* (cont.)

Directions: Read Passage A and respond to the questions below.

1 Name three other foods that can be politely eaten with one's fingers.

_____

_____

2 Make up a "it depends," using *measurable/immeasurable* or *logical/ illogical*.

_____

_____

_____

_____

. . . .

Directions: Read Passage B and respond to the questions below.

1 Do you think people should be concerned about this "immortal" jellyfish? Why?

_____

_____

_____

2 What might be some long-term effects of the "reorganization" of the world's oceans?

_____

_____

_____

_____

_____

3 Of the negative words in Passage B, which one (or more) is a synonym (has the same meaning as) for the word *unlikely*?

_____

_____

_____

Name: _____   Date: _____

What a Negative Predicament!

Directions: Match each negative phrase in Column A with the situation depicted in Column B.

Column A	Column B
1 _____ illegible scrawl	**A.** These deities never die.
2 _____ incredible news	**B.** Your thoughts make no sense.
3 _____ improper attire	**C.** I cannot eat this slop.
4 _____ unacceptable homework	**D.** I cannot read your handwriting.
5 _____ immortal gods	**E.** You acted like a child.
6 _____ inedible mess	**F.** No one could believe the shocking report.
7 _____ insoluble substance	**G.** I am wearing the wrong kind of clothes.
8 _____ unchallenged candidate	**H.** The teacher refused to take my assignment because I did not follow the directions.
9 _____ illogical thinking	**I.** This substance will not dissolve in water.
10 _____ immature behavior	**J.** No one else is running for this office.

Prefix *re-*

Standards: Uses word origins and derivations to understand word meaning (McREL 2.0)
Uses a variety of sentence structures to expand and embed ideas (McREL 2.3)
Uses conventions of spelling in written compositions (McREL 3.9)
Uses basic elements of structural analysis to decode unknown words (McREL 4.0)
Draws conclusions and makes inferences based on explicit and implicit information in texts (McREL 7.5)

Materials

- *Divide and Conquer: Prefix re-* (page 66)

- *Combine and Create: Prefix re-* (page 67)

- *Read and Reason: Prefix re-* (pages 68–70)

Teaching Tips

- Prefixes influence the meaning of a word by negating it, providing direction, or adding emphasis.

- The prefix *re-* is a directional prefix meaning "back, again." It is the second most common prefix in English, used in over 3,400 words.

- The prefix *re-* attaches to whole words (e.g., *rewrite, redo, resubmit*) and to bases that are not intact words (e.g., *revise, remit, recession, reject*).

Guided Practice

Activate Background Knowledge

1. Review the concept of a *prefix* (unit added to the front of a word that influences its meaning). Tell students that *re-* is a directional prefix meaning "back" or "again."

2. Point out that we often combine the ideas of "back" and "again." When we *rewrite* a paper, we go "back" and write it "again." When we put a car in *reverse* gear, we go "back again" over the same spot. This is why many *re-* words include the idea of repetition (again).

3. Write the words *turn*, *read*, and *build* on the board. Point out that each word can be changed with the prefix *re-*. Then, add *re-* to each word. Working with partners or in whole-class discussion, ask students to tell what each *re-* word means. Then, ask them to explain how the prefix changes the meaning. (*Return* means to "turn back" or "again" to a place you have already been.) Adding *re-* changes the meaning by adding the direction of "back, again."

4. Ask students to brainstorm more words with the *re-* prefix. Record students' responses. Ask them to pick a word from the list, tell what it means, and explain how *re-* changes the meaning of the original word.

5. Point out that *re-* attaches to whole words but also to word parts called *bases*. Write *reject* on the board. Put a slash between *re* and *ject* (*re/ject*). Tell students that *ject* is not an intact word; it is a base meaning "throw." Ask someone to explain what *reject* means ("throw" "back" and refuse to accept or keep).

Prefix *re-* *(cont.)*

Guided Practice *(cont.)* · · · · · · · · · · · · · ·
Divide and Conquer

6. Distribute copies of the *Divide and Conquer: Prefix re-* activity sheet (page 66) to students. Guide students through the activity. The sheet may be duplicated for each student and/or projected on a projector. As each word is completed, ask a student to explain what it means.

7. Explain to students that the first five words in the Divide and Conquer activity present the prefix *re-* attached to an intact word, and indicate that something is done "again" (e.g., build-rebuild, write-rewrite). Guide students through the first word, *rewrite*, by asking: "If 'write' means 'put words on paper,' and *re-* means 'back, again,' then *rewrite* means 'to write again.' (The answer is B; revise a story or write it again.)

8. The last five words present the prefix attached to a base, whose meaning is provided in the second blank. You may wish to guide students through word six, *reverse*, by asking, "If *verse-* means 'turn' and *re-* means 'back, again,' then *reverse* means to 'turn back.' Which definition in the Answer Bank has this meaning?" (The answer is E; turn back.) Working with the meaning of the base, guide students to select the best answer from the Answer Bank (e.g., to *retract* a statement is to take it "back" or with-"draw" it; to *revolve* is to spin or "roll" "again and again" repeatedly). Remember that the base provides the word's core meaning.

Combine and Create

9. Distribute copies of the *Combine and Create: Prefix re-* activity sheet (page 67) to students. Ask students to work in pairs or independently and examine *re-* words in context as they place the correct words in the blanks. After students have written their own sentences using the leftover pair(s) of *re-* words, ask them to share their sentences with classmates. Ask them to explain or describe how each *re-* word means "back" or "again." Using, hearing, and even talking about new words is an important part of learning them.

Read and Reason

10. Distribute copies of the *Read and Reason: Prefix re-* activity sheets (pages 68–70) to students. Have students read one or both passages and answer the comprehension questions. If the passages are too difficult for independent reading, ask students to read in pairs or follow along as you read aloud. Tell them to raise their hands when they hear a word beginning with the prefix *re-*. Circle the words they identify. After you have finished reading, return to each of the circled words and ask volunteers to explain their meaning. Then, invite students to answer the questions.

> **Extend and Explore**
> Choose from among the activities located on the Teacher Resource CD to give students extra practice with words beginning with the prefix *re-*.

Prefix *re-* (cont.)

Answer Key ·····················

Divide and Conquer: Prefix *re-* (page 66)

1. rewrite: back, again; write; B
2. react: back, again; act; J
3. recharge: back, again; charge; H
4. rearrange: back, again; arrange; I
5. rebuild: back, again; build; C
6. reverse: back, again; turn; E
7. retract: back, again; pull, draw, drag; D
8. rehydrate: back, again; hydrate; F
9. reject: back, again; throw, cast; G
10. revolve: back, again; roll, spin; A

Combine and Create: Prefix *re-* (page 67)

1. reported/retract
2. rejected/reinvestigate
3. refresh/rehydrating
4. reconcile/reconnecting
5. restrain/remove

Sentences will vary.

Read and Reason: Prefix *re-* (pages 68–70)

Passage A: *retraced, renew, repeat, reviewed, revisited, recalling, returned, reconsider, reacted, rebounding, reentry, recurring*

1. 10 words
2a. recalling
2b. repeat
2c. retraced

Passage B: *rebuilding, reporters, relocate, repair, reacted, response, rescue, reconsidered, restored, readjusted*

1. Answers will vary.
2. Answer will vary.
3. Answers will vary. See list above.

Name: _____   Date: _____

Divide and Conquer: Prefix *re-*

Directions: Break apart each word below. Write the prefix and its meaning in the first column. For words 1–5, write the base word in the next column. For words 6–10, the base and its meaning are provided. Combine the meanings of the prefix and the base word/base means, and select the definition from the Answer Bank. An example has been done for you.

Answer Bank
A. spin or turn repeatedly
B. revise a story or write it again
C. build something again
D. withdraw or take back (statement)
E. turn back
F. hydrate again or remoisten
G. refuse to accept
H. charge again
I. arrange again
J. act in response

word	prefix means	base word/base means	definition
❶ rewrite	re- = back, again	write	B
❷ react			
❸ recharge			
❹ rearrange			
❺ rebuild			
❻ reverse		vers- = turn	
❼ retract		tract- = pull, draw, drag	
❽ rehydrate		hydr- = water	
❾ reject		ject- = throw, cast	
❿ revolve		volv- = roll, spin	

Name: _____ Date: _____

Combine and Create: Prefix *re-*

Directions: Fill in the blanks below by choosing the pairs of *re-* words from the Word Bank. Select the paired words that make sense in the context. Two pairs of words will be left over from the bank. Write your own sentence, using at least one pair of the leftover *re-* words.

Word Bank
rejected/reinvestigate
restrain/remove
reported/retract
relocate/rearrange
refresh/rehydrating
reconcile/reconnecting
review/revise

1 Because the story had not been _____ accurately, the newspaper had to _____ it.

2 The guilty verdict was _____ by the judge, so the police had to _____ the crime.

3 It was so hot that the runner had to _____ himself by stopping frequently and _____ with a bottle of water.

4 Although they had quarreled years before, the two brothers were able to _____ and enjoy _____ with each other.

5 Police worry when a mob is angry because they are hard to _____ or _____ peacefully.

My sentence using one pair of leftover *re-* words is:

_____

_____

_____

_____

Name: _____   Date: _____

Read and Reason: Prefix *re-*

Directions: Read the passages. Circlce the words with the prefix *re-*. Then, answer the questions on page 70.

Passage A

Lost and Found

Jim retraced his steps. He must have missed something. He needed to find that ring! His mother and father were going to renew their wedding vows in two hours. They would repeat their vows in front of 200 of their closest friends and family. Without the ring, the ceremony would be ruined! In his mind, Jim reviewed everything he had done that afternoon. He revisited the places he had been, recalling his every action at the spots to which he returned. Finally, he sat on the steps to reconsider his options. Suddenly, he heard a plink-plink-pling sound, and he reacted with a start! At that very moment, the ring rolled down the stairs and hit the wall, rebounding and coming to a halt. Jim leaped up and snatched the ring.

Read and Reason: Prefix *re-* *(cont.)*

Passage B

Rebuilding Haiti

On January 12, 2010, a huge earthquake destroyed much of Haiti, the poorest country in the Western Hemisphere. The quake was centered approximately 15 miles from Haiti's capital, Port-au-Prince. According to reporters, at least 100,000 people were killed, and nearly two million people who had been left homeless were forced to relocate to new shelters. The Haitian government

estimated that 250,000 residences and 30,000 commercial buildings either collapsed or were damaged beyond repair.

People across the world reacted to the news with compassion and concern. The first response to the disaster was to rescue those trapped in the rubble and to provide food, water, and shelter to the injured. Unfortunately, many of these efforts had to be reconsidered because health, transportation, and communication systems in the capital could not be restored in time. Plans were readjusted as more humanitarian aid began to arrive in Haiti.

After the earthquake, many people slept in the streets, on patches of grass, or in cars because their houses had been destroyed. Despite efforts to rebuild, reentry into once-damaged buildings has been very gradual. In fact, many people prefer to live in make-shift "towns" made of tents and tarps, even months after the quake. Since these tent-towns do not have running water or sewage disposal, illness has now become a recurring problem. In July 2010, nearly 98 percent of the rubble from the quake remained.

Many people have shared ideas about how to begin reconstruction. However, Haitian officials have decided that the first tasks will be to rebuild downtown Port-au-Prince and to reconstruct a new government center. All involved agree that many humanitarian problems remain in Haiti; some wonder if the country can ever rebound.

Read and Reason: Prefix *re-* (cont.)

Directions: Read Passage A and respond to the questions below.

❶ How many words in Passage A begin with the prefix *re-?* _____

❷ Select the *re-* words from Passage A that best fit these definitions:

   a. bringing "back" to mind and remembering: _____

   b. (they) would say "again": _____

   c. (he) went "back again" over his tracks: _____

· ·

Directions: Read Passage B and respond to the questions below.

❶ Do you think government officials should push people out of the "tent towns" or let people live where they want to live? Why?

_____

_____

_____

❷ Do you agree with Haitian officials' plans to begin reconstruction? Why?

_____

_____

_____

❸ Find five *re-* words in the passage. Divide and conquer each.

word	prefix means	word means

Prefix *pre-*

Standards: Uses word origins and derivations to understand word meaning (McREL 2.0)
Uses a variety of sentence structures to expand and embed ideas (McREL 2.3)
Uses conventions of spelling in written compositions (McREL 3.9)
Uses basic elements of structural analysis to decode unknown words (McREL 4.0)
Draws conclusions and makes inferences based on explicit and implicit information in texts (McREL 7.5)

Materials

- *Divide and Conquer: Prefix pre-* (page 74)
- *Combine and Create: Prefix pre-* (page 75)
- *Read and Reason: Prefix pre-* (page 76–78)

Teaching Tips

- The directional prefix *pre-* means "before." It means "before" in time (e.g., *predate, prehistoric, pregame, prevent*), indicating something that occurs "before" something else. The prefix *pre-* can also mean "before" in space (e.g., a *prefix* is placed "before" the rest of the word; to *preside* at a meeting is to "sit" "before, in front of" the other members).

- The prefix *pre-* attaches to intact words (e.g., *preheated, preview*) and to Latin bases (e.g., *prejudice, predict, prepare*).

Guided Practice

Activate Background Knowledge

1. Write the word *prefix* on the board. Review the concept of a *prefix* (unit added to the front of a word that influences its meaning). Put a slash between *pre* and *fix* (*pre/fix*). Tell students that *pre-* means "before." Ask someone to explain how the concept of "before" is in the word *prefix*. (A *prefix* is "fixed" or attached "before" the base or main part of a word.)

2. Write the word *predict* on the board. Put a slash between *pre* and *dict* (*pre/dict*). Tell students that *dict* is a Latin base that means "to say" or "to tell." Ask someone to explain how the concept of "before" is in the word *predict*. (A person who predicts something "tells" about it "before" it happens.) Explain that *pre-* attaches to intact words and Latin bases.

3. Working with partners, ask students to brainstorm more *pre-* words. Record students' responses on the board. Then, ask each partner to pick a word from the list, tell what it means, and explain how adding *pre-* changes the meaning.

Divide and Conquer

4. Distribute copies of the *Divide and Conquer: Prefix pre-* activity sheet (page 74) to students. Guide students through the activity. The sheet may be duplicated for each student and/or projected on a projector. As each word is completed, ask a student to explain what it means. Make sure the definition makes sense.

Prefix *pre-* *(cont.)*

Guided Practice *(cont.)* · · · · · · · · · · · · ·

5. Explain to students that the first five words in the Divide and Conquer activity present the prefix *pre-* attached to an intact word (e.g., *view/preview*, *mixed/premixed*). Guide students through the first word, *preview*, by asking: "If *view* means 'to look at,' and *pre-* means 'before,' then *preview* means to… view before." (The answer is H; to look at in advance.)

6. Continue explaining that the last five words present the prefix attached to a base, whose meaning is provided in the second blank. You may wish to guide students through the sixth word, *predict*, by asking, "If *dict-* means 'say, tell' and *pre-* means 'before,' then *predict* means to 'say or tell before' [something happens]. Which definition in the Answer Bank has this meaning?" (The answer is A; to prophesy or forecast.) Working with the meaning of the base, guide students to select the best answer from the Answer Bank (e.g., to *precede* means to "go" "before" something; a doctor writes a *"prescription"* "before" you can get the medicine from a pharmacist). Remember that the base provides the word's core meaning.

Combine and Create

7. Distribute copies of the *Combine and Create: Prefix pre-* activity sheet (page 75) to students. Ask students to work in pairs or independently as they consider these *pre-* words in context. Then, ask students to share their answers and explain why they chose each word for the blank. Ask them to explain how each *pre-* word means "before." Using, hearing, and talking about new words is an important part of learning them.

Read and Reason

8. Distribute copies of the *Read and Reason: Prefix pre-* activity sheets (pages 76–78) to students. Have students read one or both passages and answer the comprehension questions. If the passages are too difficult for independent reading, ask students to read in pairs or follow along as you read aloud. Tell them to raise their hands when they hear a word beginning with the prefix *pre-*. Circle the words they identify. After you have finished reading, return to each of the circled words and ask volunteers to explain their meaning. Then, invite students to answer the questions.

> **Extend and Explore**
> Choose from among the activities located on the Teacher Resource CD to give students extra practice with words beginning with the prefix *pre-*.

Prefix *pre-* (cont.)

Answer Key ········

Divide and Conquer: Prefix *pre-* (page 74)

1. preview: before; view; H
2. prejudge: before; judge; C
3. premixed: before; mix; I
4. precaution: before; caution; D
5. prepaid: before; paid; F
6. predict: before; tell; A
7. prepare: before; produce; B
8. prescription: before; write; J
9. prenatal: before; birth; G
10. precede: before; move; E

Combine and Create: Prefix *pre-* (page 75)

1. prevention
2. preside
3. prefixes
4. prefer
5. prepositions
6. predictions
7. pretest
8. prescribed
9. preceded
10. prejudiced

Read and Reason: Prefix *pre-* (pages 76–78)

Passage A: *preparation, prevent, prevention, predict, prepare, precautions, prepack, premixed*

1. Answers will vary.

2. Answers will vary.

Passage B: *prehistory, precedes, predates, prehistoric, prefer, prehuman, predecessors, preliterate, preconceptions, prehistorians*

1. Answers will vary.

2. Answers will vary.

3. Answers will vary.

Name: _____ Date: _____

Divide and Conquer: Prefix *pre-*

Directions: Break apart each word below. Write the prefix and its meaning in the first column. For words 1–5, write the base word in the next column. For words 6–10, the base and its meaning are provided. Combine the meanings of the prefix and the base word/base means and select a definition from the Answer Bank. An example has been done for you.

Answer Bank
A. to prophesy or forecast
B. to make ready
C. to form an opinion or judgment before considering the facts
D. a measure taken to prevent a disaster
E. to go before
F. paid in advance
G. occurring before childbirth
H. to look at in advance
I. previously mixed
J. a written direction for medication

word	prefix means	base word/base means	definition
1 preview	pre- = before	view	H
2 prejudge			
3 premixed			
4 precaution			
5 prepaid			
6 predict		dict- = say, tell	
7 prepare		par- = produce	
8 prescription		script- = write	
9 prenatal		nat- = born, birth	
10 precede		ced- = go, move	

Name: _____   Date: _____

Combine and Create: Prefix _pre-_

Directions: Complete each sentence with the best _pre-_ word from the Word Bank below.

Word Bank				
prescribed	prepositions	preside	prefixes	prevention
preceded	prejudiced	prefer	predictions	pretest

1 An ounce of _____ is worth a pound of cure.

2 Who will _____ over this meeting?

3 _In-_, _re-_, and _pre-_ are all examples of Latin _____.

4 Would you _____ potatoes or rice?

5 Words like _to_, _for_, and _from_ are all examples of English _____.

6 The people dismissed him as a false prophet since his _____ never came true.

7 The teacher gave a _____ so that we could practice for the final examination.

8 The doctor _____ plenty of fluids and lots of bed rest.

9 The huge earthquake was _____ by several days of minor tremors.

10 Many _____ people form negative opinions of others just by looking at them.

Name: _____   Date: _____

Read and Reason: Prefix *pre-*

Directions: Read the passages. Circle the words with the prefix *pre-*. Then, answer the questions on page 78.

Passage A

Preparation Is Key

What is the best way to overcome problems? Prevent them from happening in the first place! Have you ever heard the saying "An ounce of prevention is worth a pound of cure?" Preparation means thinking ahead and trying to predict what things will help a situation. It also means thinking about what might go wrong. For instance, how would you prepare for a trip to the water park? Think about what you will need: a swimsuit, a towel, and sunscreen. So, start by packing those. Next, think about possible problems that might arise, and take the necessary precautions. You could prepack a lunch so that you would not need to carry much money to the park in order to buy food. If you do not have time to cook, you could always buy some premixed sandwich spread.

Read and Reason: Prefix *pre-* (cont.)

Passage B

Prehistory

Prehistory is the time before recorded history—that is, the long period that precedes written records. Prehistory, in other words, predates reading and writing. Names for the various prehistoric stages depend on scientists' training. Those who focus on our human ancestors think of prehistory in three stages that are named for the tools people used: Stone Age, Bronze Age, and Iron Age. Geologists, on the other hand, prefer to use the names of rock strata to define prehuman time periods.

Prehistory is actually a new science. It began in the mid-19th century, when scientists first discovered evidence of prehistoric people—sharp-edged stone tools and fossilized human bones. Since then, many scientists have joined together to solve mysteries related to very early human life. Our predecessors were preliterate, so they did not leave any written record. In a sense, then, prehistory is anonymous.

When fossilized human remains are discovered, how do scientists decide what the people looked like? At one time, scientists basically guessed, a process that tended to incorporate preconceptions about the past. Now, however, prehistorians use anatomic science and sculptural techniques to produce more accurate images of prehistoric people.

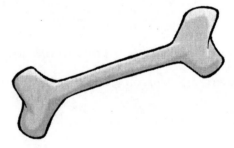

Read and Reason: Prefix *pre-* (cont.)

Directions: Read Passage A and respond to the questions below.

❶ Select three words from this list, and explain how the prefix *pre-* means "before."

_____

_____

_____

_____

❷ The word *prefix* includes the prefix *pre-*. Does this make sense? Why, or why not?

_____

_____

_____

_____

· ·

Directions: Read Passage B and respond to the questions below.

❶ Does the word *prehistory* fit its definition? Why?

_____

_____

_____

❷ Why might guesses about what early people looked like incorporate preconceptions?

_____

_____

_____

❸ List four words in Passage B that start with the prefix *pre-*. Select two words from the list, and explain how the prefix *pre-* means "before."

_____	_____
_____	_____

_____

_____

Prefixes *ex-*, *e-*, and *ef-*

Standards: Uses word origins and derivations to understand word meaning (McREL 2.0)
Uses a variety of sentence structures to expand and embed ideas (McREL 2.3)
Uses conventions of spelling in written compositions (McREL 3.9)
Uses basic elements of structural analysis to decode unknown words (McREL 4.0)
Draws conclusions and makes inferences based on explicit and implicit information in texts (McREL 7.5)

Materials

- *Divide and Conquer: Prefixes ex-, e-,* and *ef-* (page 82)

- *Combine and Create: Prefixes ex-, e-,* and *ef-* (page 83)

- *Read and Reason: Prefixes ex-, e-,* and *ef-* (pages 84–86)

Teaching Tips

- Prefixes influence the meaning of a word by negating it, providing direction, or adding emphasis.

- The prefixes *e-*, *ex-*, and *ef-* are directional prefixes meaning "out." All three forms have the same meaning.

- The form *ex-* is the most common (e.g., *exhale*, *excess*, *export*, *extend*). The assimilated spelling *ef-* occurs when the base of the word begins with the letter *f* (e.g., *effect*, *efficient*, *effort*). The form *e-* occurs when the base of the word begins with certain consonants (e.g., *erupt*, *eject*, *emission*, *edict*).

- **Note:** When the prefix *ex-* is joined with a hyphen to an intact word, it often means "former, no longer." An *ex-friend* is a former friend. This lesson deals only with nonhyphenated words beginning with the prefixes *ex-*, *e-*, and *ef-*.

Guided Practice

Activate Background Knowledge

1. Review the concept of a *prefix* (unit added to the front of a word that influences its meaning). Tell students that *ex-* is a prefix meaning "out." Write the word *exit* on the board. Ask someone to explain the meaning of the word *exit*.

2. Write the word *exhale* on the board. Ask students to inhale and then exhale. Ask where the meaning of "out" is in the word *exhale*. Put a slash between *ex* and *hale* (*ex/hale*). Explain that *ex-* attaches to many Latin bases and that *hale* means "breathe." Remind them that the base (*hale*) carries the main meaning, so *exhale* means to "breathe out."

3. Write the following sentence on the board and read it to students: *Some American-made products are exported to other countries.* Put a slash between *ex* and the base *port* (*ex/port*). Now ask students to jot down a definition for the word *exported*. Tell them to make sure they use the meaning of the prefix in their definition. Ask volunteers to share their definitions and to explain how they developed them.

4. Explain to students that *port* means "carry," so *export* means "carry out." Point out that although they may not have known the meaning of the base *port*, they could figure the word out by using *both* the meaning of the prefix and the context of the sentence.

Prefixes *ex-*, *e-*, and *ef-* *(cont.)*

Guided Practice *(cont.)* ·············

5. Write the words *erupt*, *exhaust*, and *effort* on the board. Point out that the prefix can be spelled as *e-*, *ex-* or *ef-*, depending on the next letter in the word. Ask students to talk with each other about each word, using "out" in their explanations. Then, have them share their answers with the class (a volcano breaks "out" when it *erupts*; *exhaust* fumes come "out" of cars; when we are *exhausted*, we say we are tired "out"; when we make an *effort*, we try hard and energy comes "out" of us).

Divide and Conquer

6. Distribute copies of the *Divide and Conquer: Prefixes ex-, e-, and ef-* activity sheet (page 82) to students. Guide students through the activity. The practice sheet may be duplicated for each student and/or projected on a projector. You may wish to guide students through the first word, *expire*, by asking, "If *(s)pire-* means 'breathe' and *ex-* means 'out,' then *expire* means to 'breathe out.' Which definition in the Answer Bank has this meaning?" (The answer is G; to die, breathe one's last breath, or come to an end.) Working with the meaning of the base, guide them into selecting the best answer from the Word Bank.

Combine and Create

7. Distribute copies of the *Combine and Create: Prefixes ex-, e-, and ef-* activity sheet (page 83) to students. Ask students to match each *ex-* phrase in Column I with its most appropriate speaker in Column II. Give students an opportunity to share their answers with the class because talking about and hearing new words is an important part of learning them. Encourage students to use the word *out* as they talk about words beginning with the prefixes *e-*, *ex-*, and *ef-*.

Read and Reason

8. Distribute copies of the *Read and Reason: Prefixes ex-, e-, and ef-* activity sheets (pages 84–86) to students. Have students read one or both passages and answer the comprehension questions. If the passages are too difficult for independent reading, ask students to read in pairs or follow along as you read aloud. Tell them to raise their hands when they hear a word beginning with the prefixes *e-*, *ex-*, *ef-*. Circle the words they identify. After you have finished reading, return to each of the circled words and ask volunteers to explain their meaning, using "out." Then, invite students to answer the questions.

···
: **Extend and Explore**
: Choose from among the
: activities located on the Teacher
: Resource CD to give students
: extra practice with words
: beginning with the prefixes *e-*,
: *ex-*, and *ef-*.
···

Prefixes *ex-*, *e-*, and *ef-* (cont.)

Answer Key ⋯⋯⋯⋯⋯⋯⋯

Divide and Conquer:
Prefixes *ex-*, *e-*, and *ef-* (page 82)

1. expire: out; breathe; G
2. emit: out; send; C
3. excavate: out; dig, hollow; A
4. extract: out; pull; B
5. eruption: out; break; H
6. effort: out; strength, strong; D
7. exclamation: out; shout; E
8. excursion: out; run, go; F
9. erode: out; gnaw, eat; J
10. expel: out; push; I

Combine and Create: Prefixes *ex-*, *e-*, and *ef-* (page 83)

1. D
2. F
3. H
4. G
5. J
6. I
7. E
8. C
9. A
10. B

Read and Reason: Prefixes *ex-*, *e-*, and *ef-* (pages 84–86)

Passage A: *exciting, explosives, extends, explain, expanse, explode, evacuate, exposing, exhausting, expresses, explosion, emerge, extent, exterior, explosive*

1. Answers will vary. See list above.
2a. evacuate
2b. exterior
2c. expanse

Passage B: *eruption, erupted, ejecting, explosion, evacuate, escape, extinct, expected, exclaiming, extinguish, exhausted, exhilarated, event, excursion, expedition, extract, expired*

1. **erupt:** to break out
   evacuate: to empty out
   escape: to get out of danger
   explosion: to blow out
2. Answers will vary.

Name: _____   Date: _____

Divide and Conquer: Prefixes *ex-*, *e-*, and *ef-*

Directions: Break apart each word below. Write the prefix and its meaning in the first column after the word. In the next column, the base and its meaning are provided. Combine the meanings of the prefix and base and select a definition from the Answer Bank. An example has been done for you.

Answer Bank
A. to dig or hollow out
B. to remove by pulling
C. to give off (fumes)
D. an exertion or attempt, a putting out of force or energy
E. a loud cry
F. an outing or field trip
G. to die, breathe one's last breath, or come to an end
H. sudden explosion or breaking out
I. to push out with force or to drive away
J. to wear away gradually by the action of wind or water

word	prefix means	base means	definition
❶ expire	ex- = out	(s)pire = breathe	G
❷ emit		mit- = send	
❸ excavate		cav- = dig, hollow	
❹ extract		tract = pull	
❺ eruption		rupt- = break	
❻ effort		fort- = strength, strong	
❼ exclamation		clam- = shout	
❽ excursion		curs- = run, go	
❾ erode		rod- = gnaw, eat	
❿ expel		pel- = push	

Name: _____   Date: _____

Combine and Create:
Prefixes *ex-*, *e-*, and *ef-*

Directions: Match each phrase in Column I with its most appropriate speaker in Column II. Each phrase in Column I contains the prefixes *e-*, *ex-*, or *ef-*, and each statement in Column II contains the word "out."

Column I	Column II
❶ _____ eject button	**A.** I am the motto of the United States of America: "*Out* of many, one."
❷ _____ vanilla extract	**B.** I am what you need to plug in your lamp to a faraway outlet. I stretch *out* the electrical wire.
❸ _____ royal edict	**C.** I am what you watch on TV to learn things: my shows teach and lead you *out* of ignorance!
❹ _____ effervescent personality	**D.** I am what you push to get your DVD *out* of the player.
❺ _____ side-effects	**E.** We are all the goods shipped *out* of the country for sale abroad.
❻ _____ exclusive interview	**F.** I am the oily, flavorful essence pulled *out* of the vanilla bean.
❼ _____ export products	**G.** Enthusiasm and liveliness bubble *out* of my personality!
❽ _____ educational program	**H.** I am the decree spoken *out* by a king to all his subjects.
❾ _____ e pluribus unum	**I.** I am a discussion granted to only one journalist: all others are shut *out*.
❿ _____ extension cord	**J.** I am all the other symptoms that come *out* when you take certain medications.

Name: _____   Date: _____

Read and Reason:
Prefixes *ex-*, *e-*, and *ef-*

Directions: Read the passages. Circle the words with the prefixes *ex-*, *e-* and *ef-*. Then, answer the questions on page 86.

Passage A

An Exciting Job!

Joe Frederickson is a member of the bomb squad. He specializes in explosives. His knowledge extends to a wide range of areas. He can explain some very difficult ideas about physics, chemistry, and safety. He is a good public spokesperson.

The bomb squad owns a wide expanse of land. They use the land to explode things safely in order to run tests. Right after setting the items in place, all squad members quickly evacuate the area. They must avoid exposing themselves to danger. They enter a bunker where they can be safe. Sometimes, the rush to get inside the bunker can be exhausting!

Joe makes presentations to the public about the bomb squad's work. He expresses the feelings of most of the squad members. "After an explosion, we emerge from the bunker. We inspect the extent of the blast. Whenever the exterior of the bunker is damaged, we know we have a problem. We must tone down the amount of explosive material in our formula."

Read and Reason:
Prefixes *ex-, e-,* and *ef-* (cont.)

Passage B

The Eruption of Mt. Vesuvius

Mt. Vesuvius, near the city of Naples in Southern Italy, is the only active volcano on the European mainland. The volcano erupted on August 24, AD 79, ejecting so much volcanic ash and mud that it destroyed the ancient cities of Pompeii, Herculaneum, and Stabiae. The top of the mountain was blown off by the explosion.

An ancient writer named Pliny the Younger witnessed the eruption and wrote two letters about it. He describes how the residents of the area were rushing to evacuate the city and escape the rain of flames and the rivers of hot mud. Some people had believed that the volcano was extinct, and they never expected it to erupt. Stunned by the explosion, many began crying out loud, exclaiming that the end of the world was at hand. Houses began burning, and it was impossible to extinguish the flames. Pliny himself, only 17 years old at the time, writes that his mother became exhausted while trying to flee. The air was so thick with ash and soot that it was almost impossible to inhale and exhale.

But Pliny's uncle, a natural historian named Pliny the Elder, felt exhilarated by the event and wanted to make a scientific record of the eruption. While others were fleeing, he wanted to see the spectacle from up close and planned an excursion to sail into the nearest harbor to get a better look and record the data. But when he suddenly learned that a woman who was a family friend was trapped in a villa at the foot of the volcano, Pliny the Elder abandoned his research expedition and made every effort to extract his family friend from danger. Unfortunately, the rescue mission failed. Overcome by sulfur and the flying ash and cinders, the old man Pliny expired on the spot.

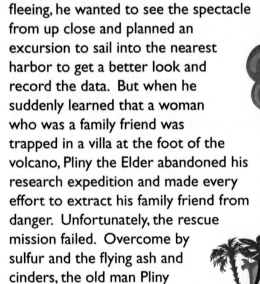

Read and Reason:
Prefixes *ex-, e-,* and *ef-* (cont.)

Directions: Read Passage A and respond to the questions below.

❶ List at least five words that begin with the prefixes e- or ex- in the passage.

_____

_____

_____

❷ Which of the e- or ex- words in the passage mean:

a. to go "out" of an area quickly, to flee: _____

b. the "outer" side of something: _____

c. a large area that spreads "out": _____

. . . .

Directions: Read Passage B and respond to the questions below.

❶ Explain what the following words mean by using the word "out" in your explanation: *erupt, evacuate, escape, explosion.*

erupt: _____

evacuate: _____

escape: _____

explosion: _____

❷ Do you think that Pliny the Elder was a brave man? Explain your answer.

_____

_____

_____

_____

_____

_____

_____

_____

Prefix *sub-* and Its Assimilated Forms

Standards: Uses word origins and derivations to understand word meaning (McREL 2.0)
Uses a variety of sentence structures to expand and embed ideas (McREL 2.3)
Uses conventions of spelling in written compositions (McREL 3.9)
Uses basic elements of structural analysis to decode unknown words (McREL 4.0)
Draws conclusions and makes inferences based on explicit and implicit information in texts (McREL 7.5)

Materials

- *Divide and Conquer: Prefix sub- and Its Assimilated Forms* (page 90)

- *Combine and Create: Prefix sub- and Its Assimilated Forms* (page 91)

- *Read and Reason: Prefix sub- and Its Assimilated Forms* (pages 92–94)

Teaching Tips

- Prefixes influence the meaning of a word by negating it, providing direction, or adding emphasis.

- The prefix *sub-* is a directional prefix meaning "under" or "below." The prefix may describe the physical idea of "below, under" (e.g., a *subfloor* lies physically "below" the floor covering; *subterranean* rivers literally flow "beneath" the earth's surface).

- The prefix *sub-* may also describe the figurative idea of "under" or "lower" in importance (e.g., a *subordinate* holds a "lower" rank than a superior; the *subplot* of a novel or film is a "lower" or "under" plot of the main plot; a *substitute* teacher holds a rank "below" the regular teacher).

Teaching Tips *(cont.)*

- Ending with the consonant *b*, the prefix *sub-* assimilates into many forms that result in doubled consonants: to *suppress* (originally *sub + press*) is to "press" "under, below"; to *succeed* (originally *sub + ceed*) is to "come" up from "under" and thereby win or accomplish something; to *suffer* (originally *sub + fer*) is to "bear" "under" and endure. Other examples of assimilated *sub-* words are *suggest*, *surrender*, and *support*.

- *Spelling Hint:* when a word begins with *su-* followed by a doubled consonant, it most likely begins with assimilated *sub-*.

- It is important to remember that the base, not the prefix, provides a word's main meaning. Some prefixes attach to whole words as well as bases.

Guided Practice

Activate Background Knowledge

1. Review the concept of a *prefix* (unit added to the front of a word that influences its meaning). Tell students that *sub-* is a prefix meaning "under" or "below." Write the word *submarine* on the board. Ask someone to explain the meaning of "under" or "below" in the word *submarine* (a boat that moves "under" or "below" the surface of the water). You might want to tell students that *marine* means "sea," so a *submarine* is a boat that travels "under" the surface of the "sea."

Prefix *sub-* and Its Assimilated Forms (cont.)

Guided Practice (cont.) ·············

2. Write the following words on the board: *subway, subtitle, substitute,* and *submerge.* Ask students to pick one of the *sub-* words and write a sentence using the word on scratch paper. Ask them to trade sentences with a neighbor. Tell them to read the sentence their neighbor wrote and write a definition of the *sub-* word. Tell them to make sure they use the words "under" or "below" in their definition. Remind them that they can use the meaning of the prefix and the sentence context to help figure out the meaning of the word. Ask volunteers to share their definitions.

3. Explain that many *sub-* words include a doubled consonant near the beginning. A *support* (*sub + port*) "carries" a weight from "below"; to *suppress* (*sub + press*) is to "press" something and hold it "below, under"; when we *suffer* (*sub + fer*), we are "under" a burden.

Divide and Conquer

4. Distribute copies of the *Divide and Conquer: Prefix sub- and Its Assimilated Forms* activity sheet (page 90) to students. Guide students through the activity. The activity sheet may be duplicated for each student and/or projected on a projector. You may wish to guide students through the first word, *submerge,* by asking, "If *merg-* means 'plunge, dip ' and *sub-* means 'below, under,' then *submerge* means to 'dip or plunge' [something] 'under.' Which definition in the Answer Bank has this meaning?" (The answer is C; to dip or plunge under water.)

Combine and Create

5. Distribute copies of the *Combine and Create: Prefix sub- and Its Assimilated Forms* activity sheet (page 91) to students. Ask students to work in pairs to combine the prefix *sub-* (including its assimilated forms) to the words and word parts in the Word Bank. Ask them to write each completed *sub-* word in the blank that best fits the described situation. Finally, ask students to share their responses with the class, explaining how each *sub-* word means "under" or "below."

Read and Reason

6. Distribute copies of the *Read and Reason: Prefix sub- and Its Assimilated Forms* activity sheets (pages 92–94). Have students read one or both passages and answer the comprehension questions. If the passages are too difficult for independent reading, ask students to read in pairs or follow along as you read aloud. Tell them to raise their hands when they hear a word beginning with the prefix *sub-* or one of its assimilated forms. After you have finished reading, return to each of the circled words and ask volunteers to explain their meaning.

> **Extend and Explore**
> Choose from among the activities located on the Teacher Resource CD to give students extra practice with words beginning with the prefix *sub-* (including its assimilated forms).

Prefix *sub-* and Its Assimilated Forms *(cont.)*

Answer Key · · · · · · · · · · · · · · · · · · ·

Divide and Conquer: Prefix *sub-* and Its Assimilated Forms (page 90)

1. submerge: under, below; plunge, dip; C
2. subtitles: under, below; title; H
3. subtract: under, below; pull, draw, drag; G
4. suppress: under, below; press; I
5. subservient: under, below; serve; D
6. subscription: under, below; write; E
7. support: under, below; carry; J
8. suffocate: under, below; throat; B
9. substandard: under, below; standard; F
10. subterranean: under, below; Earth; A

Combine and Create: Prefix *sub-* and Its Assimilated Forms (page 91)

1. subway
2. subnormal
3. submit
4. subtract/subtraction
5. substitute
6. subdivide/subdivision
7. suffix
8. subcontinent
9. subspecies
10. sublease/sublet

Teaching Hint: a *substitute* teacher stands in for a teacher, just as an "understudy" stands in for a performer. The prefix *sub-* describes the substitute's status as "under" the assigned teacher.

Read and Reason: Prefix *sub-* and Its Assimilated Forms (pages 92–94)

Passage A: *submarine, subzero, supports, subway, subordinates, success, subside, suburbs*

1. no
2. cold (below zero)
3. under water because *sub* means "below" and *marine* means "sea"

Teaching Hint: *support* means to "carry, hold" up "from under"; *success* means a "coming" up "from under"; to *subside* means to settle at a lower "level" of intensity.

Passage B: *submarine, submersible, support, submerged, succumb, suffocation, submersion, supposed*

1. They all describe an act or state where someone or something is "under" or "below."
2. Submarine sandwiches are named after the shape of the bun, whose length and rounded ends resemble a submarine.
3. Answers will vary.
4. Answers will vary.

Teaching Hint: to *succumb* means to weaken "under" a power or temptation and give way to it; *suffocation* refers to placing one's jaws or throat "under" an object that cuts off air; to *suppose* means to posit an "underlying" assumption; to *submerge* means to plunge and hold "under" water.

Name: _____   Date: _____

Divide and Conquer:
Prefix *sub-* and Its Assimilated Forms

Directions: Break apart each word below. Write the prefix and its meaning in the first column after the word. In the next column, the base and its meaning are provided. Combine the meanings of the prefix and base and select a definition from the Answer Bank. An example has been done for you.

Answer Bank
A. underground; beneath the earth's surface
B. to choke; to deprive of air
C. to dip or plunge under water
D. submissive and slavish
E. standing order for a magazine, "undersigned" by the reader
F. below par; of inferior quality
G. to reduce by taking away a number or quantity
H. captions running beneath a picture or screen
I. to hold and keep down; to keep something from emerging
J. to uphold

word	prefix means	base means	definition
1 submerge	sub- = below, under, lower	merg- = plunge, dip	C
2 subtitles		title = title	
3 subtract		tract- = pull, draw, drag	
4 suppress		press = press	
5 subservient		serv- = serve	
6 subscription		script- = write	
7 support		port- = carry	
8 suffocate		foc- = throat	
9 substandard		standard = standard	
10 subterranean		terr- = Earth	

Name: _____   Date: _____

Combine and Create:
Prefix *sub-* and Its Assimilated Forms

Directions: Work with a partner to combine the prefix *sub-* (including its assimilated forms) with the following words or word parts. Write each completed *sub-* word in the blank that best fits the described situation.

Sub- + _____				
normal	continent	species	lease or let	fix
divide or division	way	tract or traction	stitute	mit

The situation is...	The sub- word is...
❶ New York City has an elaborate underground transit system.	
❷ My body temperature has been below normal.	
❸ We need to turn in our assignment to the teacher no later than Friday.	
❹ 4 − 2 = 2	
❺ Our teacher is out sick today, so someone else will take her place.	
❻ First, we divided the pizza into four slices. Then, we cut each piece in half to make eight servings.	
❼ The word-ending *–ology* is often placed at the end of the word (*Hint:* suf-).	
❽ Greenland is a huge land mass, but not large enough to qualify as a continent.	
❾ Under the large heading of "Terrier," there are many different variations of the species, such as Scottish Terriers, Fox Terriers, Boston Terriers, and West Highland Terriers.	
❿ We leased our apartment not from the property owner but from the current renters.	

Name: _____   Date: _____

Read and Reason:
Prefix *sub-* and Its Assimilated Forms

Directions: Read the passages. Circle the words with the prefix *sub-* and its assimilated forms. Then, answer the questions on page 94.

Passage A

A New Adventure

Bweeee-op! Bweee-op! The dive sirens were blaring. The little submarine was going even deeper under the arctic ice. The subzero waters were only liquid because the salt kept them from freezing solid. And water, not ice, was important because water supports life.

Captain Hirsch was eager to explore. Just think, one month ago she had been riding the subway to her job at the aquarium! Now she was on the adventure of a lifetime, seeking life in the ocean waters of the Arctic Sea. Already, she and her subordinates had discovered a new kind of squid. And they had found two crab species not thought to live in cold waters. The crew was proud of this success.

Sometimes, she did miss home. But, she knew the homesickness would subside quickly. Her home in the suburbs would be there when she got back. This was the time for discovery!

Read and Reason:
Prefix *sub-* and Its Assimilated Forms *(cont.)*

Passage B

Submarines

A submarine is a watercraft capable of independent operation below the water's surface. It differs from a submersible, which has more limited underwater capability. The word *submarine* was originally an adjective meaning "under the sea," so some uses of the term (e.g., *submarine engineering*) do not refer to the vessel. In fact, submarines were once called submarine boats. Today, many people refer to them as *subs*.

Submarines vary in size. Some hold only one or two people, while others can hold hundreds and support life for months at a time. Some can remain submerged for only a few hours; others can remain submerged for up to six months. Submarines were once propelled by diesel-electric power. In the 1950s, nuclear power became an option, and equipment was developed to extract oxygen from seawater. In this way, the people inside the vessels did not succumb to suffocation. These two innovations lengthened submersion times and enabled lengthy voyages such as crossing the North Pole beneath the Arctic ice cap (1958). People once supposed that such voyages were impossible. Today, submerged endurance is limited only by food supply and crew morale in the space-limited submarine.

Although the first submersible boats were tools for exploring under water, inventors soon recognized their military potential. Military submarines were first widely used during World War I. German subs, called U-boats, were more submersible than true submarines. They operated primarily on the surface using regular engines, submerging occasionally to attack under battery power. A concealed military submarine is a real threat. Because of its stealth, a sub can force an enemy navy to waste resources searching large areas of ocean and protecting ships against attack.

Civilian uses for submarines include marine science, salvage, exploration, and facility inspection/maintenance. Submarines can also be modified to perform more specialized functions such as search-and-rescue missions or undersea cable repair. Submarines are employed, too, in tourism and for undersea archaeology. Scientists, military personnel, and even tourists have benefitted from innovations to the "submarine boat."

Read and Reason:
Prefix *sub-* and Its Assimilated Forms *(cont.)*

Directions: Read Passage A and respond to the questions below.

1 List all the words from Passage A that include the prefix sub-. Are there any words that do not refer to something being "under" or "below"?

_____

_____

_____

2 Are *subzero* waters cold or warm? How can you tell?

_____

_____

3 Where does a submarine travel? How can you tell?

_____

_____

· ·

Directions: Read Passage B and respond to the questions below.

1 Explain how the words *submerge*, *support*, and *succumb* mean "under" or "below."

_____

_____

_____

2 How do you think the popular "submarine sandwiches" or "subs" are related to submarine boats?

_____

_____

3 Do you think modern submarines are better suited for war or for science? Why?

_____

_____

_____

4 Why might crew morale be a concern for submarine crews?

_____

_____

Prefixes *co-* and *con-*

Standards: Uses word origins and derivations to understand word meaning (McREL 2.0)
Uses a variety of sentence structures to expand and embed ideas (McREL 2.3)
Uses conventions of spelling in written compositions (McREL 3.9)
Uses basic elements of structural analysis to decode unknown words (McREL 4.0)
Draws conclusions and makes inferences based on explicit and implicit information in texts (McREL 7.5)

Materials

- *Divide and Conquer: Prefixes co- and con-* (page 98)

- *Combine and Create: Prefixes co- and con-* (page 99)

- *Read and Reason: Prefixes co- and con-* (pages 100–102)

Teaching Tips

- Prefixes can influence the meaning of a word by negating it, providing direction, or adding emphasis.

- The prefixes *co-* and *con-* provide direction and mean "with" or "together."

- The prefixes *com-* and *col-* are assimilated forms of *con-* (see page 6) and also mean "with, together." These assimilated forms are presented in Unit III, Lesson 12. You may wish to teach these lessons in sequence.

- The prefixes *co-* and *con-* attach to whole words and to bases that are not intact words. In general, *co-* attaches to whole words (e.g., *cooperate, coworker, coauthor, cosign*), and *con-* attaches to bases (e.g., *conduct, congregate, convene*).

Guided Practice

Activate Background Knowledge

1. Review the concept of a *prefix* (unit added to the front of a word that influences its meaning). Tell students that *co-* and *con-* are prefixes meaning "with" or "together." Write the words *coworker* and *conductor* on the board. Ask someone to explain the meaning of "with" or "together" in each of those words. (A *coworker* is someone who "works" "with" you. A *conductor* is someone who "leads" a group of musicians "together" as they play music.)

2. Write the following words on the board: *coincidence, cooperate, Congress, contract*. Explain to students that you are going to read definitions of the words written on the board and they are to figure out which word each one describes. Use the following definitions:

   - **coincidence**—two things that are not planned but just happen "together"

   - **cooperate**—to work "together" or "with" others on a project

   - **Congress**—people working "together" in the state or federal Capital to make laws

   - **contract**—a business agreement that draws two or more partners "together" on a project

3. Ask students to provide examples of a *coincidence* or *cooperation* drawn from their own experiences. After each example, ask students to describe how "with" or "together" describes that experience.

Prefixes *co-* and *con-* (cont.)

Guided Practice (cont.) • • • • • • • • • • • •

Divide and Conquer

4. Distribute copies of the *Divide and Conquer: Prefixes co- and con-* activity sheet (page 98) to students. Guide students through the activity. The practice sheet may be duplicated for each student and/or projected on a projector. You may wish to guide students through the first word, *contraction*, by asking, "If *tract-* means 'pull, draw, drag' and *con-* means 'with, together,' then *contraction* means a 'pulling or drawing together.' Which definition in the Answer Bank has this meaning?" (The answer is E; an abbreviated spelling; also, the drawing together of a muscle.) Working with the meaning of the base, guide students to select the best answer from the Answer Bank.

Combine and Create

5. Distribute copies of the *Combine and Create: Prefixes co- and con-* activity sheet (page 99) to students. Ask students to work individually or in pairs. Explain that they will add the prefix *con-* to the partial words listed in the bank. Then, they will write out the entire *con-* word in the blank next to the most fitting statement. Ask students to share their answers with the class because using, hearing, and talking about new words is an important part of learning.

Read and Reason

6. Distribute copies of the *Read and Reason: Prefixes co- and con-* activity sheets (pages 100–102) to students. Have students read one or both passages and answer the comprehension questions. If the passages are too difficult for independent reading, ask students to read in pairs or follow along as you read aloud. Tell them to raise their hands when they hear a word beginning with the prefixes *co-* or *con-*. Students should circle the words they identify. After you have finished reading, return to each of the circled words and ask volunteers to explain their meaning. Then, invite students to answer the questions.

> **Extend and Explore**
> Choose from among the activities located on the Teacher Resource CD to give students extra practice with words beginning with the prefixes *co-* and *con-*.

Prefixes *co-* and *con-* (cont.)

Answer Key ······················

Divide and Conquer Prefixes *co-* and *con-* (page 98)

1. contraction: with, together; pull, draw; E
2. coagulate: with, together; drive; D
3. connect: with, together; tie; H
4. coauthor: with, together; author; C
5. consensus: with, together; think, feel; I
6. congregate: with, together; flock, herd; B
7. construct: with, together; build; J
8. container: with, together; hold, keep; F
9. cooperate: with, together; work; A
10. contagious: with, together; touch; G

Combine and Create Prefixes *co-* and *con-* (page 99)

1. convert
2. conjunction
3. conservationist
4. constellation
5. conspirator
6. conductor
7. conflagration
8. congressman

Read and Reason Prefixes *co-* and *con-* (pages 100–102)

Passage A: *conference, cofounders, company, convention, Con, congregate, converge, comingle, connect, coworkers, confer, construction, contracts, cooperative, coauthor*

1. Answers will vary. See list above.
2a. contracts
2b. conventions
2c. coauthor

Passage B: *constitutional, convention, continental, Congress, convened, cowrite, cooperation, constructing, continuous, continuity, conflict, cooperate* (**Note:** the words *comprehensive, committees, complex, compromise,* and *completely* begin with *com-*, an assimilated form of *con-*.)

1. Answers will vary.
2. Answers will vary. Accept responses expressing the general idea of "with/together." *Cooperate* = *co-* + *oper-*: "to work *together*" and get along *with* others. *Convene* = *con-* + *ven-*: "to come *together*" in a meeting or gathering to meet *with* others.

Picking the Best Prefix (page 103)

1. c
2. b
3. b
4. a
5. a
6. b
7. d

Teaching Hint: The word *constitution* consists of *con-* + the Latin base *stit-*, which means to "set up, cause to stand, establish." The Constitution is the body of laws, rules, and principles which have been "set up" together as "established" and "set" policy.

Name: _____   Date: _____

Divide and Conquer: Prefixes *co-* and *con-*

Directions: Break apart each word below. Write the prefix and its meaning in the first column after the word. In the next column, the base and its meaning are provided. Combine the meanings of the prefix and base and select a definition from the Answer Bank. An example has been done for you.

Answer Bank
A. to get along with others while working
B. to gather together in worship or ceremony
C. to write a text with someone else; a partner in writing
D. to thicken, come together, or congeal (such as blood or other liquids)
E. an abbreviated spelling; also, the drawing together of a muscle
F. a receptacle
G. catching; communicable by contact or touch
H. to join, bind, or tie together
I. agreement
J. to make or form by combining parts

word	prefix means	base means	definition
❶ contraction	con- = with, together	tract- = pull, draw	E
❷ coagulate		ag- = drive	
❸ connect		nect- = tie	
❹ coauthor		author = author	
❺ consensus		sens- = think, feel	
❻ congregate		greg- = flock, herd	
❼ construct		struct- = build	
❽ container		tain- = hold, keep	
❾ cooperate		oper- = work	
❿ contagious		tag- = touch	

Name: _____   Date: _____

Combine and Create:
Prefixes *co-* and *con-*

Directions: Add the prefix *con-* to the partial words listed below. Then, write out the entire word in the blank next to the most fitting statement.

Con- + _____			
stellation	junction	servationist	gressman
vert	spirator	ductor	flagration

I am...	The word is...
1 someone who changed religion to go with a different group of believers	
2 a connecting word in a phrase, like *and* or *but*	
3 someone who works to preserve forests and keep all things in the environment together, safe, and sound	
4 a cluster of stars in the sky	
5 someone who plots evil deeds with partners in crime	
6 someone who waves a baton in front of a symphony orchestra to make the musicians play music together	
7 a raging fire that burns a lot of things piled together	
8 a legislator who works with other elected officials	

Name: _____ Date: _____

Read and Reason: Prefixes *co-* and *con-*

Directions: Read the passages. Circle the words with the prefixes *co-* and *con-*. Then, answer the questions on page 102.

Passage A

The Game-Maker's Conference

Years ago, only a few people played video games. Today, nearly everyone does. Several years ago, cofounders of a game company started GameMakeCon. This yearly convention, called The Con, draws more people every year.

Game makers and game players congregate at The Con. They converge to share ideas. They talk about the future of gaming. Some people dress as their favorite game characters. They comingle with other players. They connect with others to learn more about their favorite games.

Others work at the meetings. Coworkers may confer about game construction. Some sign contracts to design new games, often with others. Cooperative teams coauthor many games.

Do you like video games? Whether you are a game player or would-be game maker, you would enjoy The Con.

Read and Reason: Prefixes *co-* and *con-* (cont.)

Passage B

The Constitutional Convention

The Revolutionary War was over. The new nation now needed to govern itself. Some laws had been developed in the Articles of Confederation during the Second Continental Congress in 1776. Although a good start, these rules were not comprehensive. They allowed the new government to issue money, for example, but not raise it. Moreover, the Articles did not address details about government.

To address these problems, a Constitutional Convention was convened. The 55 delegates met in Philadelphia for more than four months in 1787 to cowrite a constitution. Some wanted to revise the Articles of Confederation. Others wanted to form a totally new government. The result was the United States Constitution, which makes the Constitutional Convention among the most significant events in U.S. history. It is an amazing example of political cooperation.

The delegates needed to establish a framework for constructing and governing the new nation. This became a very thorny issue. Major plans proposed a bicameral legislature, but how should these houses of Congress be elected? Should members hold single or continuous terms of service? Should they serve for life to provide continuity of representation? Who should elect or appoint the "executive"? What kinds of powers should the nation have? The states? Should representation be proportional?

The idea of proportional representation raised another issue—what to do about slaves. Should slaves be included in population counts? Should they be subject to taxation? The conflict among delegates from the Northern and Southern states was so heated that several Southern states refused to cooperate with the Union if slavery was not allowed.

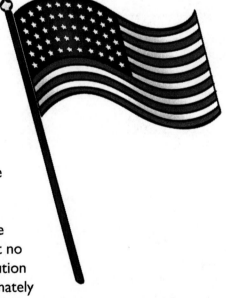

Committees were formed to explore these complex issues, and ultimately compromise won the day. Not all the delegates were pleased with the results. In some cases, communication broke down: 13 delegates left before the signing ceremony, and three of those remaining refused to sign. Thirty-nine delegates signed the Constitution, but it is likely that no one was completely satisfied. Still, the new Constitution was submitted to the states for ratification and ultimately became a framework for the new nation's governance.

Read and Reason: Prefixes *co-* and *con-* *(cont.)*

Directions: Read Passage A and respond to the questions below.

❶ List five words from the passage that begin with the prefix *co-* or *con-*.

_____

_____

_____

❷ Which of the *co-* or *con-* words in the passage have the following meanings?:

  a. agreements which business partners draw up "together":

_____

  b. large meetings of organizations which come "together" in a single city:

_____

  c. to write a book or program "together with" someone else:

_____

....

Directions: Read Passage B and respond to the questions below.

❶ What are the advantages of proportional representation? What are the disadvantages?

_____

_____

_____

❷ Divide and conquer the words *cooperate* and *convene*. You may use a dictionary for help in identifying the base of each word. Write your findings below.

Cooperate:

_____

_____

_____

Convene:

_____

_____

_____

Name: _____   Date: _____

Picking the Best Prefix

Directions: Select the best word that completes each sentence. The correct word begins with the prefix indicated within the quotation marks in each sentence. You will repeat some prefixes in your answers.

re- = back, again	pre- = before	e-, ex-, ef- = out
sub- + its assimilated forms = under, below	co-, con- = with, together	

❶ The Weather Channel is _____ rain for the Memorial Day Weekend, although we still have 10 days to go "before" the holiday.

    a. resounding   b. subjecting   c. predicting   d. presiding

❷ You can quickly suffer from frostbite by _____ your fingers to subzero temperatures. Do not put your fingers "out" in the cold air!

    a. composing   b. exposing   c. supposing   d. imposing

❸ All the musicians fixed their eyes on the _____ so that they could start playing at precisely the same moment. They wanted to keep perfect time "with" the maestro.

    a. constellation   b. conductor   c. congressman   d. concoction

❹ The journalist was forced to print a _____ of his earlier article after his informant was found to be a liar. The reporter had to take his story "back."

    a. retraction   b. contraction   c. distraction   d. subtraction

❺ The house collapsed because its foundation could not _____ the weight of the entire structure. The building broke apart "under" its own weight.

    a. support   b. import   c. export   d. deport

❻ The entire town had been _____ by the flood waters. It remained "under" water for three entire days.

    a. resided   b. submerged   c. preferred   d. constructed

❼ Simply push the _____ button to get the disc "out of" the player.

    a. reject   b. conjecture   c. subject   d. eject

Directional Prefixes *in-*, *im-*, and *il-*

Standards: Uses word origins and derivations to understand word meaning (McREL 2.0)
Uses a variety of sentence structures to expand and embed ideas (McREL 2.3)
Uses conventions of spelling in written compositions (McREL 3.9)
Uses basic elements of structural analysis to decode unknown words (McREL 4.0)
Draws conclusions and makes inferences based on explicit and implicit information in texts (McREL 7.5)

Materials

- *Divide and Conquer: Directional Prefixes in-, im-,* and *il-* (page 107)

- *Combine and Create: Directional Prefixes in-, im-,* and *il-* (page 108)

- *Read and Reason: Directional Prefixes in-, im-,* and *il-* (pages 109–111)

Teaching Tips

- Two sets of Latin prefixes in English words happen to be spelled alike! In Unit I, Lessons 4 and 5, we learned the negating prefix *in-* and its assimilated forms *im-*, and *il-*.

- This lesson presents directional prefixes *in-*, *im-*, and *il-*, meaning "in, on, into." There is no difference in meaning between the forms *in-*, *im-*, and *il-*. These are merely spelling variations that facilitate pronunciation.

- The directional prefixes *in-*, *im-*, and *il-* attach to many whole words (e.g., *inside, indoors, input*) and to Latin bases that are not whole words (e.g., *include, impel, illustrate*).

- As students encounter words with these prefixes, they should ask themselves, "Is this negative or directional *in-*, *im-*, or *il-*?"

Guided Practice

Activate Background Knowledge

1. Write the following word pairs on the board: *indoors/outdoors, inside/outside, import/export.* Ask for student volunteers to explain the difference between the two words in each pair (the words are antonyms). Although each word contains the same base (*doors, side, port*), their prefixes differ and make them opposite in meaning. All the words beginning with *in-* and *im-* mean "in," but those beginning with *out* and *ex* mean "out." Explain that the prefixes *in-* and *im-* are directional, meaning "in, on, into."

2. Ask students if they know another meaning for these prefixes. They may respond by recalling Lessons 4 and 5 from Unit I: words beginning with *in-*, *im-*, or *il-* can be negative. Explain that students need to think about words beginning with these prefixes and should ask themselves, "Is this word negative or directional?"

3. Guide students to review the negating prefix by asking, "If something is not visible it is _____ (invisible). If something is not possible, it is _____ (impossible). If something is not legal, it is _____ (illegal)." Write the words *invisible, impossible,* and *illegal* on the board, pointing out that these words begin with negative *in-*, *im-*, or *il-*. Stress that the negative meanings of these words come from the prefix.

Directional Prefixes *in-*, *im-*, and *il-* *(cont.)*

Guided Practice *(cont.)* ··············

4. Guide students to generate some directional *in-*, *im-*, and *il-* words. Say, "When I exhale, I breathe out, but when I breathe in, I _____ (*inhale*). When the police put someone in prison, they _____ (*imprison* or *incarcerate*) him or her." Tell them that the Latin base *luminate* means "light," and say, "When I shed light on something, I _____ (*illuminate*) it." Also ask, "When an author draws pictures in a book, he or she does what?" (*illustrates*). Write *inhale, imprison, illuminate,* and *illustrate* on the board, pointing out that these words begin with directional *in-*. Contrast these words with *invisible, impossible,* and *illegal,* which are all negative.

Assimilation Practice

5. Ask students which is easier to pronounce: *inprison* or *imprison; inport* or *import; inluminate* or *illuminate.* Explain that the prefix *in-* can change into *im-* or *il-* to make the word easier to pronounce.

6. You may wish to provide more sample words with explanations of how the prefixes *in-, im-,* and *il-* mean "in, on, into." Here are some examples: when we "write" our name "on" the inside cover of a book, we *inscribe* our name; when a medical doctor "sticks" a needle "in, into" our arm and gives us a shot, he or she gives us an *injection;* when we *insert* a coin into a vending machine, we "place" the coin "in, into" the slot; an *inspector* "looks" "into" a crime; an *importer* brings goods "into" the country.

Divide and Conquer

7. Distribute copies of the *Divide and Conquer: Directional Prefixes in-, im-,* and *il-* activity sheet (page 107) to students. Guide them through the activity. The practice sheet may be duplicated for each student and/ or projected on a projector. Starting with the first word, *include,* ask, "If the base *clud-* means to 'close' and the prefix *in-* means 'in, on, into,' then *include* means to 'close in.' Which definition in the word bank has this meaning?" (The answer is G; enclose.) Pick a few more words from the list and repeat the process.

Combine and Create

8. Distribute copies of the *Combine and Create: Directional Prefixes in-, im-,* and *il-* activity sheet (page 108) to students. Ask students to work in pairs and sort the words into Column A (directional *in-, im-, il-*) and Column B (negative *in-, im-, il-*). Students should talk with each other about the words as they assign them to the proper column. Students may continue to work in pairs, or they may work independently, as they complete the six sentences.

Directional Prefixes *in-*, *im-*, and *il-* (cont.)

Guided Practice (cont.) ··············

Read and Reason

9. Distribute copies of the *Read and Reason: Directional Prefixes in-*, *im-*, and *il-* activity sheets (pages 109–111) to students. Have students read one or both passages and answer the comprehension questions. The passages include words beginning with the directional prefixes *in-*, *im-* and *il-*. If the passages are too difficult for independent reading, ask students to read in pairs or follow along as you read aloud. Tell them to raise their hands when they hear a word with directional *in-*, *im-*, or *il-*. Circle the words they identify. After you have finished reading, return to each of the circled words and ask volunteers to explain what they mean. Then, invite students to answer the questions.

> **Extend and Explore**
> Choose from among the activities located on the Teacher Resource CD to give students extra practice with directional *in-*, *im-*, and *il-* words.

Answer Key ························

Divide and Conquer: Directional Prefixes *in-*, *im-*, and *il-* (page 107)

1. include: in, on, into; close; G
2. induct: in, on, into; lead; D
3. imprison: in, on, into; prison; I
4. illuminate: in, on, into; light; A
5. inhale: in, on, into; breathe; C
6. import: in, on, into; carry; E
7. inflate: in, on, into; blow; J
8. impose: in, on, into; put, place; F
9. inspector: in, on, into; watch, look at; H
10. immerse: in, on, into; dip, plunge; B

Combine and Create: Directional Prefixes *in-*, *im-*, and *il-* (page 108)

Column A words: *impression, illustrate, invade, insert, innate, indent*

Column B words: *inaccurate, impractical, illiterate, invincible*

1. indent
2. impression
3. insert
4. invade
5. illustrate
6. innate

Read and Reason: Directional Prefixes *in-*, *im-*, and *il-* (pages 109–111)

Passage A: *important, inscribe, impact, illustrate, insert, inside, impress, inclined*

1. Answers will vary. See list above.
2a. inscribe
2b. insert
2c. inclined

Passage B: *immigration, immigrants, inspection, including, incarcerated, import, indicate, inspectors, important, inspect, inducted*

1. Answers will vary.
2. Answers will vary.

Name: _____   Date: _____

Divide and Conquer:
Directional Prefixes *in-*, *im-*, and *il-*

Directions: Break apart each word below. Write the prefix and its meaning in the first column after the word. In the next column, the base and its meaning are provided. Combine the meanings of the prefix and base and select a definition from the Answer Bank. An example has been done for you.

Answer Bank
A. to enlighten; to shine light on something
B. to plunge into a liquid; to dip or dunk
C. to take a breath
D. to lead into an organization (e.g., a Hall of Fame, the Army)
E. to bring into a country or within borders
F. to put one thing on another
G. to enclose
H. an examiner who looks closely at things
I. to incarcerate; to place in jail
J. to fill with air

word	prefix means	base means	definition
❶ include	in- = in, on, into	clud- = close	G
❷ induct		duct- = lead	
❸ imprison		prison = prison	
❹ illuminate		lumin- = light	
❺ inhale		hal- = breathe	
❻ import		port- = carry	
❼ inflate		flat- = blow	
❽ impose		pos- = put, place	
❾ inspector		spect- = watch, look at	
❿ immerse		mers- = dip, plunge	

Name: _____ Date: _____

Combine and Create:
Directional Prefixes *in-*, *im-*, and *il-*

Directions: Work by yourself or with a partner to put the words below into the correct column. Six words are directional, and four words are negative. Use the six directional words to complete the sentences at the bottom of the page.

Word Bank				
inaccurate	impression	impractical	illustrate	invade
insert	innate	illiterate	indent	invincible

Column A	Column B
directional prefix means "in, on, into"	**negative prefix means "not"**

❶ When starting a new paragraph, you should always _____.

❷ I hope I make a good _____ when I meet my new teacher.

❸ You need to _____ a dime into the slot.

❹ The enemy could not _____ the territory because they had too few troops.

❺ I have artistic talent and want to _____ children's books when I grow up.

❻ All living creatures have an _____ desire for survival.

Name: _____ Date: _____

Read and Reason:
Directional Prefixes *in-*, *im-*, and *il-*

Directions: Read the passages. Circle the words with the prefixes *in-*, *im-*, and *il-*. Then, answer the questions on page 111.

Passage A

Friends Are Important

I want to give my best friend a book for her birthday. To make it special, I want to inscribe a quotation on the title page. My friend recently gave me an important piece of advice that had a profound impact on me. I want the quotation to illustrate how much I appreciate her help. I had first thought I would insert a gift certificate inside the book, but I was afraid she might think that I was trying to impress her with how much money I could spend. That is why I am more inclined to remove the price tag from the book and simply write a nice quotation.

Read and Reason:
Directional Prefixes *in-, im-,* and *il-* (cont.)

Passage B

Immigration Station—Ellis Island

Do you know what countries your ancestors came from? If they came from anywhere in Europe at least 75 years ago, they may have started their United States life at Ellis Island. This gateway for millions of immigrants from 1892 to 1954 is located in New York and New Jersey.

Immigrants spent several hours at the Ellis Island inspection station. They answered a series of questions including their names, occupations, and the amount of money they carried. They also had quick medical examinations. The sick were either sent home or incarcerated in the island's hospital, where more than 3,000 died. About two percent were denied admission to the United States for reasons such as having a chronic contagious disease, attempting to import illegal goods, or having a criminal background.

A myth persists that some immigrants were compelled to change their surnames as a condition of entrance. No historical records indicate that this actually happened. Inspectors used the passenger lists from steamship companies, so some names may have been recorded erroneously. Families may also have shortened their own names in order to fit more smoothly into American culture. Finally, spelling differences between immigrants' native languages and English may have resulted in name changes.

The wooden structure built in 1892 to house the immigration station burned down in 1897. The station's new main building opened in 1900. After 1954, the buildings fell into disrepair. In 1965 and 1966, Ellis Island was recognized as an important historic place. In its renovated buildings, opened in 1990, visitors can now inspect the areas where over 100 million Americans—one third of the population—were first inducted into the United States.

Read and Reason:
Directional Prefixes *in-*, *im-*, and *il-* (cont.)

Directions: Read Passage A and respond to the questions below.

❶ List the directional words that contain the prefixes *in-*, *im-*, and *il-*.

_____

_____

_____

❷ Of the directional *in-*, *im-*, and *il-* words in the passage, tell which means:

a. to write "on" a surface, to etch: _____

b. to place or put something "in, into" an object: _____

c. leaning "in" a certain direction or being intent "on" doing something: _____

. . . .

Directions: Read Passage B and respond to the questions below.

❶ Why do you think immigrants were asked about their occupations and the amount of money they carried?

_____

_____

_____

_____

_____

❷ Do you think it was wise to keep sick people out of the country? Why?

_____

_____

_____

_____

Prefixes *com-* and *col-*

Standards: Uses word origins and derivations to understand word meaning (McREL 2.0)
Uses a variety of sentence structures to expand and embed ideas (McREL 2.3)
Uses conventions of spelling in written compositions (McREL 3.9)
Uses basic elements of structural analysis to decode unknown words (McREL 4.0)
Draws conclusions and makes inferences based on explicit and implicit information in texts (McREL 7.5)

Materials

- *Divide and Conquer: Prefixes com- and col-* (page 115)

- *Combine and Create: Prefixes com- and col-* (page 116)

- *Read and Reason: Prefixes com- and col-* (pages 117–119)

Teaching Tips

- The directional prefixes *co-* and *con-* ("with, together") were presented in Unit II, Lesson 10. This lesson presents the assimilated forms of the same prefix: *com-* and *col-*. These forms are identical in meaning to the forms *co-* and *con-*.

- This lesson provides practice in assimilating prefixes. The spelling *com-* is found before bases beginning with *b* or *p*, as in *combine* ("to double together"), *compose* ("to put together"), and *companion* (originally, a partner "with" whom one shares "bread"). The spelling *col-* is used when the base of the word begins with the letter *l*, as in *collide* and *collaborate*.

- The prefixes *com-* and *col-* attach to a large number of Latin bases, generating many known words (e.g., *collect, compact*) and many that may be new (e.g., *colloquial, compile, commiserate*). All these words

Teaching Tips *(cont.)*

share a common meaning of "with, together": A *colloquialism* is the use of a word in spoken (not written) contexts, i.e., when people "speak" "together/with" one another; to *compile* facts and information is to "pile, heap" them "together"; to *commiserate* is to share "together with" someone's misery.

- *Spelling reminder:* Whenever a doubled consonant appears near the beginning of a word (*comm-, coll-*), students should divide between the doubled consonant to identify the assimilated prefix.

Guided Practice

Activate Background Knowledge

1. Review the prefixes *co-* and *con-* (from Unit II, Lesson 10) by asking students to generate some review words. Say, "Help me remember some words beginning with the prefix *con-*. Who remembers what that prefix means?"

2. Hold both hands up and bring them together as you pretend to be holding wires. Say, "I am an electrician. When I join two wires 'together,' what do I do?" (connect them). Now, pretend to be holding a box or jar, and say, "I am a jar that holds a lot of things 'together.' What am I?" (a container). Now say, "And what are these things inside the jar that are held 'together'?" (contents). If you have a textbook handy, open it to the Table of Contents and ask, "What does the word *contents* mean?" (Answer: all the information held "together" between the covers of the book; the book *contains* much information).

Prefixes *com-* and *col-* *(cont.)*

Guided Practice *(cont.)* ·············

Divide and Conquer

3. Distribute copies of the *Divide and Conquer: Prefixes com- and col-* activity sheet (page 115) to students. Guide students through the activity. The activity sheet may be duplicated for each student and/or projected on a projector. Starting with the first word, *collision*, ask, "If the base *lis-* means to 'slide' and the prefix *col-* means 'with, together,' then *collision* means to 'slip or slide together.' Which definition in the word bank has this meaning?" (The answer is C; a clash, crash, or conflict; an accident involving a moving vehicle.) Select a few more words from the list and repeat the process.

Combine and Create

4. Distribute copies of the *Combine and Create: Prefixes com- and col-* activity sheet (page 116) to students. Ask students to work individually or in pairs as they select the correct *com-* and *col-* words to complete the eight sentences. Have students share their answers with the class, and ask them to explain how each of the words means "with, together." Remember that using and hearing new words is an important part of learning them.

Read and Reason

5. Distribute copies of the *Read and Reason: Prefixes com- and col-* activity sheets (pages 117–119) to students. Have students read one or both passages and answer the comprehension questions. If the passages are too difficult for independent reading, ask students to read in pairs or follow along as you read aloud. Tell them to raise their hands when they hear a word with the prefix *com-* or *col-*. Students should circle the words they identify. After you have finished reading, return to the circled words and ask volunteers to explain what they mean. Then, invite students to answer the questions.

···································
: **Extend and Explore**
: Choose from among the
: activities located on the Teacher
: Resource CD to give students
: extra practice with *com-* and
: *col-* words.
···································

Prefixes *com-* and *col-* *(cont.)*

Answer Key

Divide and Conquer: Prefixes *com-* and *col-* (page 115)

1. collision: with, together; slide; C
2. companion: with, together; bread; G
3. compound: with, together; put; H
4. collapse: with, together; fall, slip; F
5. compose: with, together; put, place; B
6. colloquial: with, together; speak; A
7. collaborate: with, together; work; J
8. compress: with, together; squeeze; E
9. compatible: with, together; suffer, endure; I
10. combat: with, together; beat; D

Combine and Create: Prefixes *com-* and *col-* (page 116)

1. collection
2. compassionate
3. collaborate
4. compost
5. collided
6. compound
7. competition
8. complete

Students' sentences will vary, but they should use the words *composer* and *collapse*.

Read and Reason: Prefixes *com-* and *col-* (pages 117–119)

Passage A: *computer, collaboration, computers, colleagues, combine, collective, company, compatible, communications, committees, collaborate*

1. Answers will vary. See list above.
2a. compatible
2b. collaboration
2c. combine

Passage B: *college, colleagues, compiled, completing, community, complete, commission, common, comprehensive, commute, competitive*

Note: This passage also contains words beginning with unassimilated *con-*: *convenient, continuing, continue.*

1. Answers will vary.
2. Answers will vary.

Name: _____   Date: _____

Divide and Conquer:
Prefixes *com-* and *col-*

Directions: Break apart each word below. Write the prefix and its meaning in the first column after the word. In the next column, the base and its meaning are provided. Combine the meanings of the prefix and base and select a definition from the Answer Bank. An example has been done for you.

Answer Bank
A. conversational; occurring in spoken situations
B. to put together and arrange
C. a clash, crash, or conflict; an accident involving a moving vehicle
D. to oppose vigorously; to battle or fight against; also, a battle or fight
E. to subject to pressure; to squeeze tightly
F. to tumble down and fall apart
G. a close associate or partner; someone who accompanies another
H. made up of two or more parts
I. harmonious; in agreement; able to get along together
J. to work together on a project; to cooperate in an activity

word	prefix means	base means	definition
❶ collision	col- = with, together	lis- = slide	C
❷ companion		pan- = bread	
❸ compound		pound- = put	
❹ collapse		laps- = fall, slip	
❺ compose		pos- = put, place	
❻ colloquial		loqu- = speak	
❼ collaborate		labor- = work	
❽ compress		press- = squeeze	
❾ compatible		pat- = suffer, endure	
❿ combat		bat- = beat	

Name: _____ Date: _____

Combine and Create:
Prefixes *com-* and *col-*

Directions: Fill in the blanks by choosing the *com-* or *col-* word that best completes each sentence. Two words will be left over from the bank. Write two sentences, using the words you did not use from the Word Bank.

Word Bank				
compound	compost	composer	collaborate	collided
collection	complete	competition	compassionate	collapse

1 Our school took up a _____ to help the hurricane victims.

2 Our principal felt that sending money was the _____ thing to do.

3 Our teacher had us pick partners because she wanted us to _____ on our science projects.

4 Every fall, we rake the leaves in our backyard and add them to our _____ pile.

5 The two trucks _____ with one another on the ice-covered highway.

6 We readily recognize that *highway* and *sidewalk* are _____ words.

7 Let's hold a _____ to see which team can score more points.

8 The teacher returned my assignment and said that I had to _____ it before she could grade it.

My two remaining words are _____ and _____. My sentences using the other words are:

_____

_____

_____

_____

_____

Name: _____   Date: _____

Read and Reason:
Prefixes *com-* and *col-*

Directions: Read the passages. Circle the words with the prefixes *com-* and *col-*. Then, answer the questions on page 119.

Passage A

AIPS

Welcome to AIPS, the Artificial Intelligence Problem Solvers. We are a computer collaboration. That is right. Computers working together! We think of the computers as colleagues. They can solve everyday problems. When you tell us your needs, we combine our talents and come up with new solutions. Think of us as a collective genie, but without the bottle!

Why computers? Of course, computers have quick access to lots of information. Unlike people, computers never argue, which is just as important. They can always work together. These are the keys to our success. We make sure that every computer in our company is compatible with all the others. Our internal communications are excellent! We don't need committees. We don't need bosses. Our motto is, "We collaborate, so you don't have to."

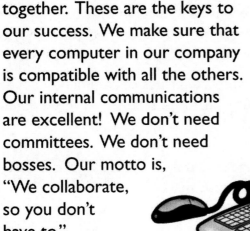

Read and Reason:
Prefixes *com-* and *col-* (cont.)

Passage B

Community Colleges

Going to school after high school takes time and costs money. Many wonder if the investment is worth it. It is. The National Center of Educational Statistics reported that college graduates earn an average of $20,000 more per year than their colleagues who graduated only from high school. Scholars have compiled many other long-term benefits of completing college.

Community colleges provide affordable and convenient post-secondary education. Most are two-year public institutions. Students who complete community college degrees either transfer to four-year institutions or move directly into the workforce.

Several historical events spurred the growth of community colleges. Laws passed in the 1860s set aside public land for occupational colleges. After World War II, the G.I. Bill enabled returning veterans to attend college. Continuing education became important, and community colleges housed these programs. In 1947, the Truman Commission called for a network of public community colleges to provide affordable education and serve community needs through a comprehensive education mission. By the end of the 20th century, community colleges were providing access to higher education, especially for people who could not otherwise afford college.

Recently, debate between the advocates and critics of community colleges has gained strength. Advocates argue that these schools serve the needs of society. Students who cannot afford to leave home to live at a four-year college can easily commute to the urban campus of a community college, and the associate degrees offered by these schools make the graduates more competitive in the job market. Critics, however, maintain that such colleges continue a culture of privilege by not allowing working class youth to advance in social class. Whether community colleges give opportunity or protect privilege, they are now a common part of higher education.

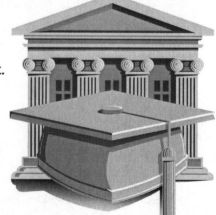

Read and Reason:
Prefixes *com-* and *col-* (cont.)

Directions: Read Passage A and respond to the questions below.

❶ List five different words from Passage A that begin with the prefixes *com-* or *col-*.

_____

_____

_____

❷ Which of the *com-* or *col-* words in the passage have these meanings?:

   a. agreeable and harmonious, getting "along with" others: _____

   b. a cooperation or a working "together" of two or more parties: _____

   c. to put two or more things "together" and mix them: _____

· ·

Directions: Read Passage B and respond to the questions below.

❶ Aside from increased income, what might be some long-term benefits of completing college?

_____

_____

_____

_____

_____

_____

❷ What is your opinion about community colleges? Do you side with advocates or critics? Why?

_____

_____

_____

_____

_____

Prefix *de-*

Standards: Uses word origins and derivations to understand word meaning (McREL 2.0)
Uses a variety of sentence structures to expand and embed ideas (McREL 2.3)
Uses conventions of spelling in written compositions (McREL 3.9)
Uses basic elements of structural analysis to decode unknown words (McREL 4.0)
Draws conclusions and makes inferences based on explicit and implicit information in texts (McREL 7.5)

Materials

- *Divide and Conquer: Prefix de-* (page 123)

- *Combine and Create: Prefix de-* (page 124)

- *Read and Reason: Prefix de-* (pages 125–127)

Teaching Tips

- The directional prefix *de-* means "down, off of."

- This prefix attaches to many whole words (e.g., *degrease, deice, defrost, dehydrate*) and to many Latin bases that are not intact words (e.g., *decapitate, descend, demote*).

- When *de-* means "off of," it describes physical removal (e.g., to *declaw* a cat is to remove its claws) or the reduction of something that has accumulated (e.g., to *deice* a windshield is to reduce or eliminate ice; to *deflate* a balloon is to let the air out).

- When *de-* means "down," it can describe a physical downward motion, as in *depressing* a button (by pushing it "down") or *descending* the stairs. It can also describe the figurative idea of "down," as in feeling *depressed* (feeling "down"), or getting a *demotion* in school (being sent "down" a grade).

Teaching Tips *(cont.)*

- The ideas of "down" and "off" are related: when things come "off" and detach, they tend to fall "down." By contrast, we say that things "stay up" when they remain attached.

- The prefix *de-* does not assimilate.

Guided Practice

Activate Background Knowledge

1. Write these three phrases on the board: *declaw a cat, deice a windshield, degrease a roasting pan.* Ask students to turn to their neighbor and discuss the words beginning with the prefix *de-*. Ask, "What do the words beginning with *de-* mean, and what do they have in common?" After a few minutes, ask for volunteers to report their answers. All answers should mention taking something "off of" something: to *declaw* a cat is to take *off* its claws; to *deice* a windshield is to take *off* the ice; to *degrease* a pan is to take *off* built-up grease. Explain that the prefix *de-* means "off of."

2. Write the following three phrases on the board: *descend the stairs, depress a button, demote to a lower grade.* Ask students to discuss these phrases with a neighbor. Ask the same question: "What do the words beginning with *de-* mean, and what do they have in common?" After a few minutes, ask for volunteers to report their answers. All answers should mention the idea of "down" or "downward motion."

Prefix *de-* *(cont.)*

Guided Practice *(cont.)* ··············

Divide and Conquer

3. Distribute copies of the *Divide and Conquer: Prefix de-* activity sheet (page 123) to students. Guide students through the activity. The activity sheet may be duplicated for each student and/or projected on a projector. Starting with the first word, *descend*, ask, "If the base *scend-* means to 'climb' and the prefix *de-* means 'down,' then *descend* means to 'climb down.' Which definition in the word bank has this meaning?" (The answer is G; to come down from above.) Select a few more words from the list and repeat the process.

Combine and Create

4. Distribute copies of the *Combine and Create: Prefix de-* activity sheet (page 124) to students. Ask students to work individually or in pairs to match the *de-* words with their definitions. Upon completion, ask students to read their answers aloud, making sure that they mention the words "down" or "off of."

Read and Reason

5. Distribute copies of the *Read and Reason: Prefix de-* activity sheets (pages 125–127) to students. Have students read one or both passages. The passages include words beginning with the prefix *de-*. If the passages are too difficult for independent reading, ask students to read in pairs or follow along as you read aloud. Tell them to raise their hands when they hear a word with the prefix *de-*. Students should circle the words they identify. After you have finished reading, return to the circled words and ask volunteers to explain what they mean. Then, invite students to answer the questions.

> **Extend and Explore**
> Choose from among the activities located on the Teacher Resource CD to give students extra practice with *de-* words.

Prefix *de-* *(cont.)*

Answer Key ·······················

Divide and Conquer: Prefix *de-* (page 123)

1. descend: down, off of; climb; G
2. dehydrated: down, off of; water; C
3. deposit: down, off of; put, place; D
4. demolish: down, off of; throw; B
5. demotion: down, off of; move; H
6. deflate: down, off of; blow; I
7. depose: down, off of; put, place; J
8. defog: down, off of; fog; E
9. depress: down, off of; squeeze, press; F
10. delouse: down, off of; louse (singular of "lice"); A

Combine and Create: Prefix *de-* (page 124)

1. I
2. A
3. J
4. B
5. H
6. E
7. D
8. C
9. F
10. G

Read and Reason: Prefix *de-* (pages 125–127)

Passage A: *descending, departed, descend, decrease, deactivate, depress, detach, deflate, deplete*

1. Answers will vary. See list above.
2a. Answers will vary. Accept responses which describe climbing down, going downstairs, the landing of a plane as it lowers itself to the ground, etc.
2b. Answers will vary. Accept responses which describe pressing or pushing down a button, a lever, etc.
2c. Answers will vary. Accept responses which describe letting air out of a balloon, the air coming out of or "off" of it, its coming down to the ground, etc.
3. Answers will vary. Accept responses which describe feeling down, not feeling up to doing things, being down in the mouth, down in the dumps, being called a downer, etc.

Passage B: *defend, dehydration, depleted detrimental, defined, deficient, destructive, dependent, defenseless, detect*

1. Answers will vary.
2. Answers will vary.

Name: _____   Date: _____

Divide and Conquer: Prefix *de-*

Directions: Break apart each word below. Write the prefix and its meaning in the first column after the word. In the next column, the base and its meaning are provided. Combine the meanings of the prefix and base and select a definition from the Answer Bank. An example has been done for you.

Answer Bank
A. to free of lice; to remove lice from
B. to destroy
C. drained or deprived of water or moisture
D. to put down for safekeeping
E. to clear; to remove mist or haze
F. to press down; to lower in spirits
G. to come down from above
H. reduction to or placement in a lower class or division
I. to release air from
J. to remove from high office or a position of power; dethrone

word	prefix means	base means	definition
❶ descend	de- = down, off of	scend- = climb	G
❷ dehydrated		hydr- = water	
❸ deposit		posit- = put, place	
❹ demolish		mol- = throw	
❺ demotion		mot- = move	
❻ deflate		flat- = blow	
❼ depose		pos- = put, place	
❽ defog		fog = fog	
❾ depress		press- = squeeze, press	
❿ delouse		louse = louse (singular of "lice")	

Name: _____   Date: _____

Combine and Create: Prefix *de-*

Directions: Match each phrase in Column I with the most appropriate speaker in Column II. Every definition contains the words *down* or *off of*.

Column I	Column II
1 _____ deciduous foliage	**A.** I was the king before the people put me "down" from power.
2 _____ dethroned monarch	**B.** I have been feeling sad and "down" lately.
3 _____ dehydrated athlete	**C.** I am under 18 years old and live "off of" my parents.
4 _____ depressed individual	**D.** I am a special area where unruly students are kept "down" from acting out in disruptive behaviors.
5 _____ demolition crew	**E.** I am a town that used to thrive, but now all the people have moved "off of" this spot on the map.
6 _____ depopulated area	**F.** I am the sediment that the river has put "down" at the bottom of the riverbed.
7 _____ detention center	**G.** I can trace my family tree straight "down" the line to the first immigrants to Ellis Island.
8 _____ dependent minor	**H.** I am a team of workers who knock "down" buildings so that new ones can be built.
9 _____ fluvial deposit	**I.** I am the kind of leaves that turn brown and fall "down" in autumn.
10 _____ direct descendant	**J.** I failed to drink a lot of fluids while I was exercising, and the water in my body is way "down."

Name: _____   Date: _____

Read and Reason: Prefix *de-*

Directions: Read the passages. Circle the words with the prefix *de-*. Then, answer the questions on page 127.

Passage A

Instructions for a Model Blimp Descending

Now that your blimp has departed and has ascended into the air, you will have to bring it back down. To make your blimp descend, you must decrease the amount of gas. To do this, first deactivate the pump so no more gas is inflating the balloon. Next, depress the button on your controller. This will temporarily detach the plug at the end of the balloon. With the plug out of the way, the blimp will slowly deflate.

Caution: If you deplete your gas tank, you will not be able to reinflate the balloon.

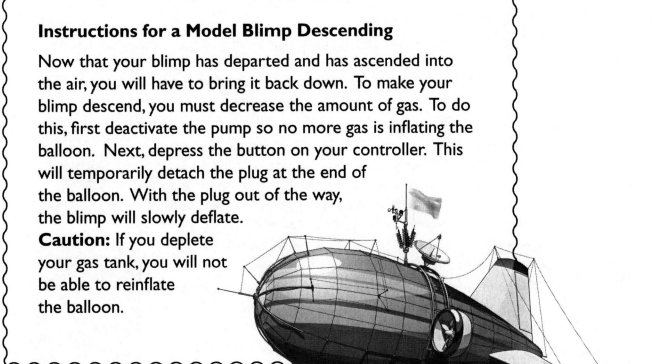

Read and Reason: Prefix *de-* (cont.)

Passage B

Defend Yourself from Dehydration

Did you know that about half your body weight consists of water? What do you suppose would happen if you lost some of that water? To lose a small amount, say through excessive perspiration, fever, or vomiting, would not be detrimental to your health. But if you lose too much, you may suffer from a dangerous condition called *dehydration*.

Dehydration is defined as mild, moderate, or severe, based on how deficient the body's fluids are. Symptoms of dehydration include a dry or sticky mouth, low urine output, not producing tears, sunken eyes, and skin that loses resiliency. Severe dehydration is destructive of overall health and can even be a life-threatening emergency.

Infants and children are more susceptible to dehydration than adults because of their smaller body weights. In addition, sick children may refuse to eat or drink, which compounds dehydration. The elderly are also at risk, and it can be difficult to detect if their bodies are depleted of essential fluids. These groups, often dependent on others for their care, may be defenseless against the ravages of dehydration.

Drinking fluids can defend against mild dehydration. Frequent small amounts of fluid are better than larger amounts. Electrolyte drinks or freezer pops can also be effective, but sugary drinks should be avoided. Moderate and severe dehydration may be treated through intravenous fluids, which requires hospitalization.

When dehydration is recognized and treated promptly, the outcome is generally good. Still, doctors advise that people should drink plenty of fluids every day. Drink more when exercising or when the weather is hot. Thirsty? Drink some water. And watch for signs of dehydration.

Read and Reason: Prefix *de-* (cont.)

Directions: Read Passage A and respond to the questions below.

❶ List at least five words in this passage that begin with the prefix *de-*.

_____

_____

_____

❷ Think about the words *descend*, *deflate*, and *decrease*. Explain how each of these words means "down":

   a. *descend*: _____

   b. *depress*: _____

   c. *deflate*: _____

❸ The word *depress* in the passage describes what to do with a button. Explain how the related word *depressed*, which means "sad," also means "down."

_____

_____

_____

· ·

Directions: Read Passage B and respond to the questions below.

❶ If you were caring for a sick child, when would you become concerned about dehydration?

_____

_____

_____

❷ What effect do you think a fever would have on dehydration? Why?

_____

_____

_____

Prefix *pro-*

Standards: Uses word origins and derivations to understand word meaning (McREL 2.0)
Uses a variety of sentence structures to expand and embed ideas (McREL 2.3)
Uses conventions of spelling in written compositions (McREL 3.9)
Uses basic elements of structural analysis to decode unknown words (McREL 4.0)
Draws conclusions and makes inferences based on explicit and implicit information in texts (McREL 7.5)

Materials

- *Divide and Conquer: Prefix pro-* (page 131)

- *Combine and Create: Prefix pro-* (page 132)

- *Read and Reason: Prefix pro-* (pages 133–135)

Teaching Tips

- The prefix *pro-* means "forward, ahead, for." Its directional force is clear in such words as *progress* (literally, a stepping "forward, ahead") and *promote* (to move "forward, ahead" to the next grade or level).

- This prefix also means "for" in the sense of "in favor of." This meaning is clear in the phrase *pros and cons.* Most students easily understand such hyphenated words as *pro-peace* ("for" peace) and *pro-environment* ("for" the environment).

- The meanings of "forward, ahead" and "for" are related: when we are "for" an idea, we move it "ahead" and *promote* it.

- The prefix *pro-* attaches to a large number of Latin bases, generating such academic words such as *proposal, procession,* and *provisions.*

- The prefix *pro-* does not assimilate. It is always spelled as *pro-*.

Guided Practice

Activate Background Knowledge

1. Draw a horizontal arrow on the board, from left to right. Beneath it, near the start of the arrow, write the words *propeller* and *projector.* Ask students what these words have in common. (Answer: They begin with the prefix *pro-*.)

2. Explain that the prefix *pro-* is "directional." Ask the following leading questions about the words:

   - When a plane is flying in the air, does the *propeller* send it forward or backward? (When they answer "forward," draw a forward-moving arrow after the word).

   - When we go to the movies, does the *projector* in the back room send the picture onto the screen forward or backward? (When they answer "forward," draw another arrow after the word.)

3. Review the words, emphasizing the arrow that indicates "forward, ahead." Announce that all words beginning with the prefix *pro-* indicate "forward, ahead" movement.

   Ask students, "If I am *pro-peace*, am I for peace or against it?" Accept their response. Now say, "If I am for saving the environment, what am I?" (Guide students to answer *pro-environment.*)

Prefix *pro-* *(cont.)*

Guided Practice *(cont.)* ·············

4. Write the hyphenated words *pro-peace* and *pro-environment* on the board. Explain that *pro-* also means "for." Ask students, "Who has ever heard of the phrase *the pros and the cons* of something?" Explain that the pros are the reasons "for" doing something. Point out that when we are "for" something, we usually write *pro-* with a hyphen before the rest of the word (as in *pro-business* policies, to be *pro-healthcare*, etc.)

5. Ask students to think about the words *noun* and *pronoun*. Explain that a noun is the name of a person, place, or thing (e.g., *boy*, *girl*). Tell students the following scenario:

   "I saw two boys fighting on the playground. I told the boys to stop."

   Now ask, "In the second sentence, what word would I use instead of *the boys*?" (Guide students to answer with the word *them*.) Explain that *them* is a pronoun, a word that "stands for a noun." Repeat that *pro-* means "for." Other pronouns that "stand-for-nouns" are: *he, she, it, him, her, they,* and *them*.

Divide and Conquer

6. Distribute copies of the *Divide and Conquer: Prefix pro-* activity sheet (page 131) to students. Guide students through the activity. The practice sheet may be duplicated for each student and/or projected on a projector. Starting with the first word, *proceed*, ask, "If the base *ceed-* means to 'go' and the prefix *pro-* means 'forward, ahead, for,' then *proceed* means to 'go ahead.'

Which definition in the word bank has this meaning?" (The answer is E; to move forward or ahead; to continue or carry on.)

7. Repeat step 6 with the word *produce*. Explain that the word has an interesting etymology: "If the base *duc-* means 'lead' and the prefix *pro-* means 'forward, ahead, for,' then *produce* is what Mother Earth 'leads forth' from the ground as fruits and vegetables. This is the original meaning of *produce*." As a verb, *produce* means to generate or "lead forward" into existence. (The answer is B; to generate or bring forth goods or products; also, fruits or vegetables brought forth from the earth.)

8. Repeat step 6 with the word *provisions*. Explain that the word has an interesting etymology: "If the base *vis-* means 'look, see,' and the prefix *pro-* means 'forward, ahead, for,' then *provisions* are what we acquire as we 'look ahead' to things we will need in the future, such as groceries for the upcoming week, which we call *provisions*." (The answer is A; supplies acquired or measures taken as a person looks ahead to upcoming needs.)

Combine and Create

9. Distribute copies of the *Combine and Create: Prefix pro-* activity sheet (page 132) to students. Ask students to work individually or in pairs to complete the five sentences with the *pro-* words provided in the list and to compose two sentences of their own, using the leftover words. Ask students to read all the sentences aloud. Then discuss the direction of "forward, ahead" in each word.

Prefix *pro-* (cont.)

Guided Practice (cont.)

Read and Reason

10. Distribute copies of the *Read and Reason: Prefix pro-* activity sheets (pages 133–135) to students. Have students read one or both passages and answer the questions. If the passages are too difficult for independent reading, ask students to read in pairs or follow along as you read aloud. Tell them to raise their hands when they hear a word with the prefix *pro-*. Students should circle the words they identify. After you have finished reading, return to each of the circled words and ask volunteers to explain what they mean. Then, invite students to answer the comprehension questions at the end of the passage.

> **Extend and Explore**
> Choose from among the activities located on the Teacher Resource CD to give students extra practice with *pro-* words.

Answer Key

Divide and Conquer: Prefix *pro-* (page 131)

1. proceed: forward, ahead, for; go; E
2. promotion: forward, ahead, for; move; J
3. protrude: forward, ahead, for; thrust, jut; D
4. propel: forward, ahead, for; push, drive; H
5. progressive: forward, ahead, for; step, go; I
6. produce: forward, ahead, for; lead; B
7. pronoun: forward, ahead, for; noun, name; F
8. provisions: forward, ahead, for; see, look; A
9. proclaim: forward, ahead, for; shout; C
10. pro-peace: forward, ahead, for; peace; G

Combine and Create: Prefix *pro-* (page 132)

1. Proclamation
2. Providence
3. propulsion
4. prolonged
5. proposal

The remaining words are *progress* and *procrastinate*. Students' sentences will vary.

Read and Reason: Prefix *pro-* (pages 133–135)

Passage A: *promising, proposal, professor, producer, project, propulsion, procedure, provide, proceed, provision, produce, product, promoting, proposals*

1. Answers will vary. See list above.
2a. *pro-* means "forward," and *pul-* means "push"
2b. *pro-* means "forward," and *duce-* means "lead". When we *produce* something, we lead it forth into being. The earth "leads forth" crops as *produce*. Accept a wide range of responses.
2c. *pro-* means "forward," and *ceed-* means "go". When we *proceed*, we "go ahead" or "move forward."
3. Answers will vary.

Passage B: *protect, profits, pronouncements, progressed, prosperous, promise, prospects, prosperity, prospectors, prospect, prolonged, provisions, provoked, proliferated, professional, promoters, produced*

1. Answers will vary.
2. Answers will vary.
3. Answers will vary.

Name: _____   Date: _____

Divide and Conquer: Prefix _pro-_

Directions: Break apart each word below. Write the prefix and its meaning in the first column after the word. In the next column, the base and its meaning are provided. Combine the meanings of the prefix and base and select a definition from the Answer Bank. An example has been done for you.

Answer Bank
A. supplies acquired or measures taken as a person looks ahead to upcoming needs
B. to generate or bring forth goods or products; also, fruits or vegetables brought forth from the earth
C. to announce; to declare openly and publicly
D. to jut forward or stick out
E. to move forward or ahead; to continue or carry on
F. a word used in place of a noun
G. in favor of peace
H. to drive forward or ahead by force; to push ahead
I. forward looking in attitude; favoring improvement and reform
J. advancement to the next grade or level

word	prefix means	base means	definition
❶ proceed	pro- = forward, ahead, for	ceed- = go	E
❷ promotion		mot- = move	
❸ protrude		trud- = thrust, jut	
❹ propel		pel- = push, drive	
❺ progressive		gress- = step, go	
❻ produce		duc- = lead	
❼ pronoun		noun = noun, name	
❽ provisions		vis- = see, look	
❾ proclaim		claim- = shout	
❿ pro-peace		peace = peace	

Name: _____   Date: _____

Combine and Create: Prefix *pro-*

Directions: Look at the box below. There are seven words that begin with the prefix *pro-*. You will use five of these words to complete the sentences below. Use the remaining two words to write at least two of your own sentences.

Word Bank			
Proclamation	proposal	Providence	propulsion
progress	procrastinate	prolonged	

① All students of American history learn that Abraham Lincoln issued the Emancipation _____.

② The capital of Rhode Island is named _____ in honor of God, who provides for humankind.

③ My dad's fishing boat has an outboard motor with jet _____.

④ Our teacher _____ the period and held us over because we had been disruptive.

⑤ I would like to make a _____ that we postpone the test until next Monday.

My sentences using the other words are:

_____

_____

_____

_____

_____

_____

Name: _____   Date: _____

Read and Reason: Prefix *pro-*

Directions: Read the passages. Circle the words with the prefix *pro-*. Then, answer the questions on page 135.

Passage A

A Promising Proposal

Greetings, Professor Lux!

I am Sam, the producer on this motion picture project. Thank you so much for helping us with our documentary on jet propulsion. Many people would like to learn how jets move!

Now, let me tell you about the procedure we will follow. First, I will provide you with a script in the morning. Once we have everything together, we will proceed with filming your demonstration. We will need to have a list of provisions you will need so that we can obtain them in advance.

Thank you for helping us produce the best possible product that we can. We have grand plans for promoting the movie, and we look forward to any future proposals you may wish to submit.

Sincerely,

Sam Caldwell

Read and Reason: Prefix *pro-* (cont.)

Passage B

The California Gold Rush

In 1848, James Marshall saw something unusual in a river running by John Sutter's sawmill. Gold! He and Sutter tried to protect their discovery. They wanted the profits from the gold for themselves. Within a few months, though, pronouncements about gold in California had reached the rest of the nation. The California Gold Rush had begun.

The term *rush* is appropriate. By 1850, California's population had increased tenfold. San Francisco suddenly progressed from a village of 1,000 to a bustling and prosperous city of 35,000. The promise of instant prosperity caused many to become prospectors. In an age when farmers were earning about a dollar a day, the prospect of making $16.00 per day in the goldfields was exciting indeed.

The promise of easy riches drew many people to California, and this changed life in many ways. The diversity of nationalities and sharp fluctuations in economic prospects kept life unsettled. Prospectors worked long hours in remote places, often living in ramshackle housing for prolonged periods of time. They paid exorbitant prices for food and provisions. Still, prospectors were willing to endure these conditions; they had "gold fever."

For a while, prospectors found gold by hand digging or sifting the silt from rivers. Miners worked to "stake their claims" and register ownership of land on which they had discovered gold, often racing to beat their competitors to the Claims Office. Such fierce competition often provoked violence, and crime proliferated in many mining camps.

After a few years, the only remaining gold was buried in veins deep inside the mountains. To extract this gold required professional ventures. Independent prospectors went home as promoters of large mining companies moved in.

The six-year California Gold Rush yielded $300 million in gold. But many who marketed supplies to the miners achieved even greater fortunes. One of these was Levi Strauss, the German immigrant who produced blue jeans and first sold them to prospectors. The Gold Rush is over, but the jeans are still making millions!

Read and Reason: Prefix *pro-*(cont.)

Directions: Read Passage A and respond to the questions below.

❶ Write five words from the passage that have the prefix *pro-*.

_____

_____

_____

❷ Explain how the following words mean "forward, ahead, for":

a. *propulsion:* _____

b. *produce:* _____

c. *proceed:* _____

❸ Write a sentence using at least two of the *pro-* words you listed above.

_____

_____

_____

. . . .

Directions: Read Passage B and respond to the questions below.

❶ Do you think the prospectors were naïve? Why or why not?

_____

_____

_____

❷ Why do you think marketers like Levi Strauss made more money during the Gold Rush than many of the miners did?

_____

_____

_____

❸ List three words with the prefix *pro-*. Divide and conquer each word. Then tell how *pro-* contributes to the meaning of each word.

_____

_____

_____

Prefixes *trans-* and *tra-*

Standards: Uses word origins and derivations to understand word meaning (McREL 2.0)
Uses a variety of sentence structures to expand and embed ideas (McREL 2.3)
Uses conventions of spelling in written compositions (McREL 3.9)
Uses basic elements of structural analysis to decode unknown words (McREL 4.0)
Draws conclusions and makes inferences based on explicit and implicit information in texts (McREL 7.5)

Materials

- *Divide and Conquer: Prefixes trans- and tra-* (page 140)

- *Combine and Create: Prefixes trans- and tra-* (page 141)

- *Read and Reason: Prefixes trans- and tra-* (pages 142–144)

Teaching Tips

- The prefixes *trans-* and *tra-*, meaning "across, change," appear in many academic words.

- These prefixes indicate the physical direction of "across." When we *transport* goods, we carry them "across" an area. When we *transmit* germs by sneezing, we send them *across* the room. Many cities have a public *transit* system of buses and trains that go "across" town. Drapes are operated by *traverse* rods, which pull them "across" the window. The word *traffic* refers to the movement of vehicles "across" an area.

- Many words with the prefixes *trans-* and *tra-* also indicate change. These words are frequently found in academic vocabulary. For example, when we accidentally switch letters, we *transpose* them by "changing" their position.

Teaching Tips *(cont.)*

- The ideas of "across" and "change" are related: when we go "across" an area, we "change" places.

- The word *travesty,* meaning mockery, expresses the idea of "change." In Medieval comedies, actors "changed" their "clothing" (*vest-* = clothing) as they donned costumes to make fun of public figures on stage. This is the origin of *travesty,* which now means "mockery, sham."

- The forms *tra-* and *trans-* do not assimilate (except in the word *traffic*).

Guided Practice

Activate Background Knowledge

1. Ask students to think about words built on the base *port-*, which means "to carry." Trigger their memory by saying, "When we carry goods into a country, we do what?" (*import*) Write *import* on the board. Now say, "When we carry goods out of a country, we do what?" (*export*) Write *export* on the board. Now say, "When we carry goods across the country, we do what?" (*transport*) Write the word *transport* on the board. Divide and Conquer it, explaining that the prefix *trans-* means "across." Write the phrase *transportation system* on the board, and ask students to talk to their neighbors about what this phrase means. Explain again that *trans-* means "across."

Prefixes *trans-* and *tra-* (cont.)

Guided Practice (cont.) ·············

2. Pretend to have a cold and pretend to sneeze without covering your mouth. Ask students if they can think of a word we use when we send our germs "across" the room. If the word *transmit* does not occur to them, ask them to turn to a neighbor and figure out what *trans-* word we use when we spread germs.

3. Write the words *transform* and *transformation* on the board. Ask for volunteers to explain what a *transformation* is. Accept their answers, and explain that *trans-* also means "change." Explain that this prefix has two forms: *trans-* and *tra-*, but they mean the same thing: "across, change."

Divide and Conquer

4. Distribute copies of the *Divide and Conquer: Prefixes trans- and tra-* activity sheet (page 140) to students. Guide students through the activity. The practice sheet may be duplicated for each student and/or projected on a projector. Starting with the first word, *transportation*, ask, "If the base *port-* means to 'carry' and the prefix *trans-* means 'across, change,' then *transportation* means the 'carrying across' of things to a changed location. Which definition in the word bank has this meaning?" (The answer is F; the conveyance of goods or people from one area to another.)

5. Repeat step 4 with the word *travesty*. Explain to students that the word has an interesting etymology: "If the base *vest-* means 'clothing' and the prefix *tra-* means 'change,' then a *travesty* is a comedy performed in 'changed' 'clothing' (costumes). This is the original meaning of *travesty*. Today, it means "mockery," as in the phrase *travesty of justice*, which describes an outrageous verdict that mocks the judicial system." (The answer is B; mockery.)

6. Repeat step 4 once again with the word *transitory*. Explain to students once again that the word has an interesting etymology: "If the base *it-* means 'go' and the prefix *trans-* means 'across, change,' then *transitory* means 'going across' and 'fleeting,' not 'staying.' We say that mortal life is transitory, fleeting, because we are 'passing through!'" (The answer is J; fleeting, ephemeral; not lasting or permanent.)

Combine and Create

7. Distribute copies of the *Combine and Create: Prefixes trans- and tra-* activity sheet (page 141) to students. Ask students to work individually or in pairs to match the phrases in Column A (all containing the *trans-* and *tra-* prefixes) with the situations depicted in Column B. When they are finished, invite students to share answers and explain how the phrases in Column A mean "change" or "across."

Prefixes *trans-* and *tra-* *(cont.)*

Guided Practice *(cont.)*

Read and Reason

8. Distribute copies of the *Read and Reason: Prefixes trans- and tra-* activity sheets (pages 142–144) to students. Have students read one or both passages and answer the questions. If the passages are too difficult for independent reading, ask students to read in pairs or follow along as you read aloud. Tell them to raise their hands when they hear a word that contains the prefixes *tra-* or *trans-*. Students should circle the words they identify. After you have finished reading, return to each of the circled words and ask volunteers to explain what they mean. Then, invite students to answer the questions.

> **Extend and Explore**
> Choose from among the activities located on the Teacher Resource CD to give students extra practice with *tra-* and *trans-* words.

Answer Key

Divide and Conquer: Prefixes *trans-* and *tra-* (page 140)

1. transportation: across, change; carry; F
2. transmit: across, change; send; G
3. transpose: across, change; put, place; D
4. trajectory: across, change; throw, cast; E
5. transcript: across, change: write; I
6. travesty: across, change; clothing; B
7. transgress: across, change; step; A
8. transparent: across, change; appearance, seem; H
9. transformation: across, change; shape, form; C
10. transitory: across, change; go; J

Combine and Create: Prefixes *trans-* and *tra-* (page 141)

1. H
2. A
3. E
4. G
5. J
6. F
7. B
8. C
9. D
10. I

Prefixes *trans-* and *tra-* (cont.)

Answer Key (cont.) ·················

Read and Reason: Prefixes *trans-* and *tra-* (pages 142–144)

Passage A: *transfer, transit, trans-Atlantic, transported, traffic, traverse, transporting, transportation*

1. The uncle lived in Europe.
2a. transport
2b. traffic
3. Answers will vary.

Passage B: *transcontinental, transportation, transactions, transformed, traversing, transit, traffic, transfer, transport*

1. Answers will vary.
2. Answers will vary.

Name that Direction! (page 145)

1. across
2. in or into
3. together
4. forward or ahead
5. together
6. into or in
7. together
8. down
9. on
10. down

Name: _____   Date: _____

Divide and Conquer:
Prefixes *trans-* and *tra-*

Directions: Break apart each word below. Write the prefix and its meaning in the first column after the word. In the next column, the base and its meaning are provided. Combine the meanings of the prefix and base and select a definition from the Answer Bank. An example has been done for you.

Answer Bank
A. violate a rule; offend a prohibition; step across the line between right and wrong
B. mockery (originally a comedy performed in costume)
C. a profound change or alteration in substance or appearance
D. to switch the order
E. the path of a moving object as it travels across an area
F. the conveyance of goods or people from one area to another
G. to deliver or dispatch; to pass on to another
H. clear, obvious; not opaque; easily seen through
I. written record of grades, official statements, or evidence
J. fleeting, ephemeral; not lasting or permanent

word	prefix means	base means	definition
❶ transportation	trans- = across, change	port- = carry	F
❷ transmit		mit- = send	
❸ transpose		pos- = put, place	
❹ trajectory		ject- = throw, cast	
❺ transcript		(s)cript- = write	
❻ travesty		vest- = clothing	
❼ transgress		gress- = step	
❽ transparent		par- = appearance, seem	
❾ transformation		form- = shape, form	
❿ transitory		it- = go	

Name: _____   Date: _____

Combine and Create:
Prefixes *trans-* and *tra-*

Directions: Match each phrase in Column A with the situation depicted in Column B.

Column A	Column B
❶ _____ blood transfusion	**A.** I wrote itno instead of into.
❷ _____ transposition of letters	**B.** We usually take the bus to go downtown.
❸ _____ transition period	**C.** I cannot read Russian, so I bought a good English version of Dostoevsky.
❹ _____ business transaction	**D.** My aunt is waiting for a donor for a new kidney.
❺ _____ traverse rods	**E.** We're going through a time when everything is changing.
❻ _____ transcontinental commerce	**F.** We enjoy a free exchange of goods between North and South America.
❼ _____ public transit	**G.** We signed a contract and bought the house.
❽ _____ reliable translation	**H.** The doctors had to change his blood before the operation.
❾ _____ organ transplant	**I.** I need to send all my high school grades to the colleges I am applying to.
❿ _____ academic transcript	**J.** Just pull the cord to draw the drapes across the rod.

Name: _____ Date: _____

Read and Reason:
Prefixes *trans-* and *tra-*

Directions: Read the passages. Circle the words with the prefixes *trans-* and *tra-*. Then, answer the questions on page 144.

Passage A

You Need a Transfer!

I wanted to save money on cab fare, and so I—foolishly—decided to take public transit from the loading dock at the New York harbor. My uncle had just sent me a large suitcase on a trans-Atlantic steamer, and I wanted to bring it home. I thought, "This suitcase has been transported all the way across the ocean. I can get it to my house on the public bus!"

But the bus did not go directly to my house. The heavy traffic made for very slow going. Then, at the end of the line, the driver told me to transfer to another bus. He explained that there was no direct route from the harbor to my house. "What?" I cried in disbelief. "Do you mean I have to traverse the entire city just to get home? I have to lug this huge case with me, transporting it all the way across town by hand! I've had it with public transportation. From now on, I'll just pay cab fare."

Read and Reason:
Prefixes *trans-* and *tra-* (cont.)

Passage B

The Transcontinental Railroad

Imagine that you lived in the 1800s and needed to get across the country from New York to California. You could take a stagecoach or ride a horse, but the trip would take months. Such slow transportation hampered transactions between eastern and western businesses. Congress studied the situation for more than a decade and finally passed a law in 1862 to build a transcontinental railroad. Workers went east from California and west from the Iowa/Nebraska border.

The project attracted many former Civil War soldiers as well as Irish and Chinese immigrants. Most of the work involved laying the rails by hand. The average daily progress was less than two feet per day.

Workers from each direction encountered problems. In the west, plans were transformed to deal with traversing the rugged Sierra Mountains. Going through the mountains required tons of dynamite and people to set the charges. The Chinese, who were willing to do this hazardous work, became the backbone of the western work crew.

Workers coming from the east encountered Native American war parties. Railroad officials responded by increasing security and hiring marksmen to kill American bison, which threatened workers and were the primary food source for the Plains Indians.

The work crews passed each other in northern Utah. No one had decided where the rails were to join. Government engineers then selected Promontory Point, Utah, for the connection. In a ceremony that included a symbolic golden railroad spike, the two lines were linked on May 10, 1869. Rapid transit between the east and west coasts was, at last, a reality!

The transcontinental railroad transformed areas around the route, which brought rapid economic growth. It served as a vital link for commerce and for transportation of all sorts of merchandise. Traffic across the country began to escalate, and passengers were easily able to transfer from one train to another as they made their way. The railroad provided faster, safer, and cheaper transport east and west for people and goods. The time required for coast-to-coast transit was reduced from six months to just one week.

Read and Reason:
Prefixes *trans-* and *tra-* (cont.)

Directions: Read Passage A and respond to the questions below.

❶ Since the suitcase had been shipped on a *trans-Atlantic* steamer, what continent do you think the uncle lived on?

_____

❷ Of the *tra-* and *trans-* words in the passage, tell which one means:

  a. to carry across: _____

  b. a congestion of cars and other vehicles moving across the city:

  _____

❸ Explain how a bus *transfer* is used to make a change.

_____

_____

_____

· ·

Directions: Read Passage B and respond to the questions below.

❶ The transcontinental railroad has been called one of the greatest technological advances of the 19th century. Do you believe it deserves this label? Why or why not?

_____

_____

_____

❷ What do you think of the railroad officials' decision to kill bison?

_____

_____

_____

Name: _____   Date: _____

Name that Direction!

Directions: Fill in the blank in each sentence with the directional word that best fits the sentence. You will use some words more than once.

Word Bank				
down	together	in, on, into	across	forward, ahead

1 I take public transit to travel _____ town because it costs less than driving.

2 Importers bring foreign goods _____ our country.

3 A musician puts notes _____ in order to compose a symphony.

4 A sales promotion aims to move a specific product _____ in the marketplace.

5 An electrician connects wires by twisting them _____.

6 The invaders rushed fearlessly _____ their neighbors' territory.

7 My stamp collection book keeps my favorite stamps _____ in one place.

8 As the airplane descended, it smoothly glided _____ toward earth to make its landing.

9 When I shed light _____ an object, I illuminate it.

10 I made a _____ payment by depositing money with the cashier.

Prefix *inter-*

Standards: Uses word origins and derivations to understand word meaning (McREL 2.0)
Uses a variety of sentence structures to expand and embed ideas (McREL 2.3)
Uses conventions of spelling in written compositions (McREL 3.9)
Uses basic elements of structural analysis to decode unknown words (McREL 4.0)
Draws conclusions and makes inferences based on explicit and implicit information in texts (McREL 7.5)

Materials

- *Divide and Conquer: Prefix inter-* (page 150)
- *Combine and Create: Prefix inter-* (page 151)
- *Read and Reason: Prefix inter-* (pages 152–154)

Teaching Tips

- This lesson presents the directional prefix *inter-*, which means "between, among." It attaches to a large number of intact words (e.g., the *Internet*, *interstate* highways, *intramural* sports) and to many Latin bases that are not whole words (e.g., *interrupt*, *interfere*, *intercept*, *interrogate*).

- This prefix is found in everyday words, in academic vocabulary, and in many words from social studies (e.g., *international*, *interfaith*, *interracial*).

- Many *inter-* words are associated with an ongoing exchange "between" things. This force is clear in such words as *Internet*, which promotes communication "between" people and *interactive* games involve a give-and-take exchange "between" the player and the video monitor.

Teaching Tips *(cont.)*

- Other *inter-* words are associated with separating and "coming between" things. When we *interrupt*, we "break between" the words of a speaking person; when we *interfere,* we meddle and come "between" people engaged in an activity; a football player *intercepts* a pass by coming "between" the thrower and the intended recipient; summer *intervenes* "between" the spring and fall semesters.

- The prefix *inter-* does not assimilate.

- *Helpful Hint:* As students Divide and Conquer *inter-* words, they should look at the entire prefix and not divide it prematurely as the prefix *in-*. They should ask themselves, "How does this word mean 'between'?"

Guided Practice

Activate Background Knowledge

1. Invite two students to the board. Ask one student to draw a street along a horizontal line. Ask the other to draw a street along a vertical line that cuts across the middle of the first street. Have one student draw a circle at the point where the two streets meet. Then ask, "Who knows a word beginning with *inter-* that describes the area where two streets cut between each other?" (*intersection*)

Prefix *inter-* (cont.)

Guided Practice (cont.) ·············

2. Write the word *intersection* on the board. Draw a slash after the letter *r* and explain that the prefix *inter-* means "between." Explain that pedestrians are to cross streets only at the intersection, since this *in-* "between" spot is the best place to see if cars are coming from any direction (the base *sect-* means "cut").

3. Ask two students to come to the board. Designate one as a journalist and the other as a celebrity, and have them face each other. Have the journalist ask the celebrity questions about his or her favorite song, hobbies, foods, friends, etc. Have the celebrity give answers. Then, stand between them, gesturing back and forth with your hand, and ask the class, "What *inter-* word do we use to describe this conversation 'between' the questioner and respondent?" (*interview*). Write the word *interview* on the board, identify the prefix, and announce that the prefix *inter-* means "between." (The base *view* means "see": we see people when we interview them face-to-face and a conversation occurs between us.)

4. Have students work in pairs or small groups and ask them to brainstorm other *inter-* words they know. Accept their answers as they call them out and write them on the board, slashing each word after the prefix *inter-* (e.g., *inter/rupt, inter/fere, Inter/net, inter/active*).

Divide and Conquer

5. Distribute copies of the *Divide and Conquer: Prefix inter-* activity sheet (page 150) to students. Guide students through the activity. The practice sheet may be duplicated for each student and/or projected on a projector. Starting with the first word, *interrupt*, ask, "If the base *rupt-* means to 'break' and the prefix *inter-* means 'between, among,' then *interrupt* means to 'break between.' Which definition in the Answer Bank has this meaning?" (The answer is F; to stop something in progress; to break the uniformity of an activity.) Select a few more words from the list and repeat the process.

Combine and Create

6. Distribute copies of the *Combine and Create: Prefix inter-* activity sheet (page 151) to students. Ask students to work in pairs or individually to match the two-word phrases in Column I with the statements quoted in Column II. Review the answers, having students read the quotations that contain the words *between* or *among*. Give students an opportunity to talk about the words, because using, hearing, and talking about new words is important to learning them.

Prefix *inter-* *(cont.)*

Guided Practice *(cont.)* ··············

Read and Reason

7. Distribute copies of the *Read and Reason: Prefix inter-* activity sheets (pages 152–154) to students. Have students read one or both passages and answer the questions. If the passages are too difficult for independent reading, ask students to read in pairs or follow along as you read aloud. Tell them to raise their hands when they hear a word with the prefix *inter-*. Students should circle the words they identify. After you have finished reading, return to the circled words and ask volunteers to explain what they mean. Then, have students answer the questions.

> **Extend and Explore**
> Choose from among the activities located on the Teacher Resource CD to give students extra practice with the prefix *inter-*.

Answer Key ·······················

Divide and Conquer: Prefix *inter-* (page 150)

1. interrupt: between, among; break; F
2. intramural: between, among; wall; G
3. intermediate: between, among; middle; D
4. intersection: between, among; cut; J
5. international: between, among; nation; I
6. interfere: between, among; bear, go; E
7. intermittent: between, among; send; B
8. interrogate: between, among; ask; C
9. intersperse: between, among; scatter; A
10. interfaith: between, among; faith, belief; H

Combine and Create: Prefix *inter-* (page 151)

1. C
2. F
3. G
4. J
5. A
6. B
7. D
8. E
9. I
10. H

Prefix *inter-* (cont.)

Answer Key (cont.) ·················

Read and Reason: Prefix *inter-*
(pages 152–154)

Passage A: *interview, interviewer, interested, interrogation, interfere, intergalactic, intervene, international, intercultural, interrupting, interject, interesting, interfaith, interracial, intercommunications, intermission*

1. Answers will vary. See list above.

2a. Anwers will vary. *Interrupt* means to break "between" people who are speaking; to break "between" the words or ongoing activity of a speaker or worker. Accept a wide range of responses.

2b. Answers will vary. *Intervene* means to come "between" two or more people or groups. Accept a wide range of responses.

2c. Answers will vary. *Interfaith* means promoting communication and dialogue "between" different religions. Accept a wide range of responses.

3. *intergalactic*

Passage B: *Internet, interconnected, international, internetwork, interconnecting, interstate, interoperability, intercommunication, interpersonal, interactions, interoffice, intergovernmental, interdependent*

1. Answers will vary. The Internet allows communication "between, among" people. It links people with connections "between, among" many parties, etc. Accept a wide range of responses.

2. Answers will vary.

3. Answers will vary.

Name: _____   Date: _____

Divide and Conquer: Prefix *inter-*

Directions: Break apart each word below. Write the prefix and its meaning in the first column after the word. In the next column, the base and its meaning are provided. Combine the meanings of the prefix and base and select a definition from the Answer Bank. An example has been done for you.

Answer Bank
A. to sprinkle or scatter; to place here and there between other things
B. occurring now and then; stopping and starting at irregular intervals; sporadic
C. to question formally or intensely
D. occurring at the midpoint; at a moderate level
E. to meddle; to come between others when not invited
F. to stop something in progress; to break the uniformity of an activity
G. occurring between different schools (as in sports)
H. involving people from different religions
I. occurring between different countries
J. a junction at which two (or more) roads or paths meet and overlap

word	prefix means	base means	definition
❶ interrupt	inter- = between, among	rupt- = break	F
❷ intramural		mur- = wall	
❸ intermediate		med- = middle	
❹ intersection		sect- = cut	
❺ international		nation = nation	
❻ interfere		fer- = bear, go	
❼ intermittent		mitt- = send	
❽ interrogate		rog- = ask	
❾ intersperse		spers- = scatter	
❿ interfaith		faith = faith, belief	

Name: _____   Date: _____

Combine and Create: Prefix *inter-*

Directions: If the two-word phrases in Column I could speak, they would match the statements spoken in Column II. Match each phrase with its most appropriate speaker. Every statement includes the word *between* or *among*.

Column I	Column II
❶ _____ intramural sports	**A.** We cut between each other. We are never parallel.
❷ _____ interlinear translation	**B.** We are discussions that promote understanding between or among different religions.
❸ _____ intercepted pass	**C.** We are football games played between two different schools.
❹ _____ musical interlude	**D.** We are scattered periods of rain that occur between short sunny periods at uneven intervals.
❺ _____ intersecting lines	**E.** I am a pact or treaty between different countries.
❻ _____ interfaith dialogues	**F.** I am a French novel, with the English version of my text printed between the lines.
❼ _____ intermittent showers	**G.** I am a football that was caught by a third player between the thrower and the intended recipient.
❽ _____ international agreement	**H.** I am a short break or recess between the parts of a long program. At baseball games, I am the seventh-inning stretch.
❾ _____ interstate highway	**I.** I am a road that runs between New Jersey and Illinois.
❿ _____ brief intermission	**J.** I am the entertainment provided by musicians between the acts of a play or opera.

Name: _____   Date: _____

Read and Reason: Prefix *inter-*

Directions: Read the passages. Circle the words with the prefix *inter-*. Then, answer the questions on page 154.

Passage A

Imaginary Interview with an Alien from Outer Space

Interviewer: Welcome back. Our guest today is Fidgi Glorp-Glorp. Mr. Glorp-Glorp, we are all interested in you. Please do not think of this as an interrogation. We simply wish to know why you have come. Are you here to interfere with Earth affairs?

Alien: Oh no! Many people may look on me as an intergalactic invader. But I have not come to intervene in human affairs. I can do nothing about international relations among your many countries. I cannot involve myself in your intercultural disputes. I simply want to…

Interviewer: Pardon me for interrupting, sir, but I am amazed by your English vocabulary. Let me interject a compliment! Many of our listeners may not know what you mean by "intercultural disputes." Could you explain?

Alien: Of course. Where I come from, we are all alike. We look the same. We even have the same thoughts and beliefs. For this reason, we have no serious conflicts or disagreements. It's kind of boring in my galaxy! Earth is so much more interesting. But disputes can be difficult. You seem to need interfaith dialogues and interracial communication. I think improved intercommunications would help you solve many problems. But, I will not interfere in human affairs.

Interviewer: I would like to ask some more questions, but first we must pause for a brief intermission. Listeners, stay tuned!

Read and Reason: Prefix *inter-* (cont.)

Passage B

The Internet

The Internet is a global system of interconnected computer networks. It connects millions of computers around the world on an international scale and beyond. *Internet* is a short form of the technical term "internetwork," which refers to interconnecting computer networks with special gateways or routers. Just as the Interstate Highway System of the 1950s improved transportation across the United States, so does the Internet bring people together on the so-called "information highway."

The Internet has no centralized policies for access, use, or technological implementation. Each constituent network sets its own standards, and networks are voluntarily interconnected. However, a corporation called ICANN maintains interoperability for the underlying core infrastructure.

The Internet has changed information gathering, communication, shopping, and even the ways in which people work. Many people now read news online, for example, so newspaper subscriptions have been affected. New forms of intercommunication are possible through instant messaging and social networking. Interpersonal communications have thus been greatly affected. Online shopping has boomed for both major retailers and small artisans. Since the Internet allows remote access to computers, working from home and business-to-business collaboration are enhanced. This affects interactions and interoffice work routines in many industries. It has also allowed intergovernmental cooperation and communication.

The Internet is becoming a powerful political tool. In 2004, presidential candidate Howard Dean demonstrated its use for organizing and fundraising. Around the world, many political groups now use the Internet to carry out their missions. In some cases, this has led to Internet censorship, but Internet activism is likely to continue to affect political movements around the world.

Internet use has grown tremendously. From 2000 to 2010, the number of Internet users globally rose from 394 million to 1.97 billion. Since the 1990s, the Internet has affected nearly all aspects of life. We are now interdependent in new ways, with additional changes likely in the future.

Read and Reason: Prefix *inter-* (cont.)

Directions: Read Passage A and respond to the questions below.

❶ Record five words from the passage that begin with the prefix inter-.

_____

_____

_____

❷ Explain how the following words mean "between, among":

a. *interrupt:* _____

_____

b. *intervene:* _____

_____

c. *interfaith:* _____

_____

❸ Which of the *inter-* words in the passage means "occurring between galaxies"?

_____

· ·

Directions: Read Passage B and respond to the questions below.

❶ How do you think the word *Internet* reflects the meaning of the prefix *inter-*?

_____

_____

_____

❷ Compare social networks to person-to-person communication. Explain the difference.

_____

_____

_____

❸ Do you think Internet-related changes are positive, negative, or both? Explain.

_____

_____

_____

Prefixes *di-*, *dif-*, and *dis-*

Standards: Uses word origins and derivations to understand word meaning (McREL 2.0)

Uses a variety of sentence structures to expand and embed ideas (McREL 2.3)

Uses conventions of spelling in written compositions (McREL 3.9)

Uses basic elements of structural analysis to decode unknown words (McREL 4.0)

Draws conclusions and makes inferences based on explicit and implicit information in texts (McREL 7.5)

Materials

- *Divide and Conquer: Prefixes di-, dif-, and dis-* (page 159)

- *Combine and Create: Prefixes di-, dif-, and dis-* (page 160)

- *Read and Reason: Prefixes di-, dif-, and dis-* (pages 161–163)

Teaching Tips

- This lesson presents the directional prefix *dis-*, which means "apart," "in different directions," "not," along with its two variant forms *di-* and *dif-*. These prefixes attach to a large number of Latin bases, generating both known words (e.g., *different, direction, digestion, dismiss*) and words that may be new (e.g., *dilapidated, disposition, disposed, dismissive, diffusion*).

- The prefix *dis-* is the most commonly encountered spelling. The assimilated form *dif-* is used when the consonant *f* follows (e.g., *differ, diffuse, diffident*). The spelling *di-* is used before the consonants *g, l, r,* and *v* (e.g., *digest, dilated, direct, divest*).

- Many words with this prefix mean "apart" and "in different directions." When a teacher *dismisses* class, students are physically sent "in different directions."

Teaching Tips *(cont.)*

- The idea of "apart" and "in different directions" can also be figurative: *distractions* pull our attention "in different directions" and do not let us concentrate; a *disruptive* student breaks the class "apart" with *distracting* behavior; when we are emotionally "shaken" "apart," we feel *disturbed*.

- The prefix *dis-* negates many whole words by meaning "not." Examples include *ability/ disability* ("not" able to do certain things); *connected-disconnected; honesty/dishonesty; infect/disinfect; similar/dissimilar.* The meanings of "apart," "in different directions," and "not" are related: when things come "apart," they cease to exist.

Guided Practice

Activate Background Knowledge

1. Write the word *dismiss* on the board. Then, ask individual students, "Where do you go after class is *dismissed*?" Draw an arrow from the word *dismiss* and aim it at the student's destination. Repeat the question with three or four more students, spoking out arrows in different directions as they answer.

2. Point to the many arrows under the word *dismiss* and explain that the prefix *dis-* means "apart" and "in different directions." Say, "When we are dismissed from school, we scatter. This direction is indicated by the prefix *dis-*, which means 'apart' and 'in different directions.'"

Prefixes *di-*, *dif-*, and *dis-* (cont.)

Guided Practice (cont.) ··············

3. Ask students, "When a policeman *directs* traffic at a busy intersection, where do the cars go?" (in different directions). Explain that the prefix *dis-* has forms spelled as *di-* and *dif-*. They also mean "apart, in different directions." Write the word *different* on the board and divide the word by inserting a slash between the two *f*s. Explain that *dif-* also means "apart, in different directions."

4. Tell students, "If you are trying out for a team or a part in a play, you can be qualified or..." (*disqualified*). Ask, "What does *dis-* mean in this word?" Explain that it means "not." Provide more examples of whole words that can be negated with *dis-*: connected wires can be *disconnected*; a person who is not honest is *dishonest*; a soldier can receive an honorable or a *dishonorable* discharge from the army; we can be satisfied with the food at a restaurant or *dissatisfied* with it; we can *disinfect* an infected area.

5. Write a few more *di-*, *dif-*, and *dis-* words on the board: *differ*, *digest*, *dislocated*. Discuss how these words mean "apart, in different directions, not."

Divide and Conquer

6. Distribute copies of the *Divide and Conquer: Prefixes di-, dif-, and dis-* activity sheet (page 159) to students. Guide students through the activity. The practice sheet may be duplicated for each student and/or projected on a projector. Explain that the prefix in the first seven words is directional, meaning "apart, in different directions." Words 8 through 10 are whole words to which the negating prefix *dis-* is attached, meaning "not."

7. Starting with the first word, *disruptive*, ask students, "If the base *rupt-* means 'to break' and the prefix *dis-* means 'apart, in different directions,' then *disruptive* means 'breaking apart.' Which definition in the Answer Bank has this meaning?" (The answer is F; causing disturbances; disorderly.)

8. Repeat step 7 with the word, *disintegrate*. Ask students, "If the base *integr-* means 'whole' and the prefix *dis-* means 'apart' and 'in different directions; not,' then disintegrate means 'to fall apart from a whole state; to not be whole.' Which definition in the word bank has this meaning?" (The answer is B; to fall apart or crumble.) Select a few more words from the list and repeat the process.

Prefixes *di-*, *dif-*, and *dis-* *(cont.)*

Guided Practice *(cont.)* ·············

Combine and Create

9. Distribute copies of the *Combine and Create: Prefixes di-, dif-, and dis-* activity sheet (page 160) to students. Ask students to work individually or in pairs as they sort the *di-*, *dif-* and *dis-* words into the two categories. Remind them that the prefix means "apart," and "in different directions," but that it also means "not." Explain to students that they can figure out the meaning by looking at the rest of the word following the prefix: when attached to a whole word, *dis-* usually means "not." Then, have students complete the four sentences, selecting from the words they have written in the first box. Have students share answers with the class, and ask them to explain how each of the words means "apart," "in different directions," or "not." Encourage talking about words and sentences because using and hearing new words is an important part of learning them.

Read and Reason

10. Distribute copies of the *Read and Reason: Prefixes di-, dif-, and dis-* activity sheets (pages 161–163) to students. Have students read one or both passages and answer the questions. If the passages are too difficult for independent reading, ask students to read in pairs or follow along as you read aloud. Tell them to raise their hands when they hear a word with the prefix *di-*, *dif-*, and *dis-*. Students should circle the words they identify. After you have finished reading, return to the circled words and ask volunteers to explain what they mean. Then, invite students to answer the questions.

···································

Extend and Explore
Choose from among the activities located on the Teacher Resource CD to give students extra practice with the prefixes *di-*, *dif-*, and *dis-*.

···································

Prefixes *di-*, *dif-*, and *dis-* (cont.)

Answer Key

Divide and Conquer: Prefixes *di-*, *dif-*, and *dis-* (page 159)

1. disruptive: apart, in different directions, not; break; F
2. dismiss: apart, in different directions, not; send; D
3. distracted: apart, in different directions, not; pull, draw, drag; I
4. different: apart, in different directions, not; bear, go; G
5. disintegrate: apart, in different directions, not; whole; B
6. direct: apart, in different directions, not; straight, guide; E
7. dispute: apart, in different directions, not; think; H
8. dishonest: apart, in different directions, not; honest; C
9. disconnected: apart, in different directions, not; connected; A
10. disinfect: apart, in different directions, not; infect; J

Combine and Create: Prefixes *di-*, *dif-*, and *dis-* (page 160)

Words meaning "apart, in different directions": *distribute, dispenser, disturbance, dilapidated, digest, disruption*

Words meaning "not": *disqualified, disreputable, dissimilar, dissatisfied, dishonorable*

Hint: Point out that the words in the second box begin with *dis-*, followed by an intact word. The words *qualified, reputable, similar, satisfied*, and *honorable* are whole words.

Sentence completions:

1. digest
2. dilapidated
3. distribute
4. disturbance

Read and Reason: Prefixes *di-*, *dif-*, and *dis-* (pages 161–163)

Passage A: *difficulty, distracted, disarray, disorder, dissatisfactory, digest, disgusting, dismiss, disreputable, discomfort, distance*

1. Answers will vary. See list above.
2a. dissatisfactory
2b. disreputable
2c. distracted
3. Sentences will vary.

Passage B: *diversity, distributed, differing, distinct, differed, discrete, dimensions, dissimilarities, different, distinguish, differ, difficult, disappearing, disuse*

1. Answers will vary.
2. Answers will vary.
3. Answers will vary. See list above.

Name: _____   Date: _____

Divide and Conquer:
Prefixes *di-, dif-,* and *dis-*

Directions: Break apart each word below. Write the prefix and its meaning in the first column after the word. In the next column, the base and its meaning are provided. Combine the meanings of the prefix and base and select a definition from the Answer Bank. An example has been done for you.

Answer Bank
A. not joined together
B. to fall apart or crumble
C. deceitful, insincere, lying, untruthful
D. to release, let go, discharge; to allow to leave
E. to regulate or guide; also, immediate and straightforward
F. causing disturbances; disorderly
G. dissimilar, not the same; unusual
H. a controversy or quarrel; a difference of opinion
I. unable to concentrate; having one's attention diverted
J. to cleanse thoroughly, to purify

word	prefix means	base means	definition
1 disruptive	dis- = apart, in different directions, not	rupt- = break	F
2 dismiss		miss- = send	
3 distracted		tract- = pull, draw, drag	
4 different		fer- = bear, go	
5 disintegrate		integr- = whole	
6 direct		rect- = straight, guide	
7 dispute		put- = think	
8 dishonest		honest	
9 disconnected		connected	
10 disinfect		infect	

Name: _____ Date: _____

Combine and Create:
Prefixes *di-*, *dif-*, and *dis-*

Directions: Sometimes the prefixes *di-*, *dif-*, and *dis-* mean "apart, in different directions," and sometimes they mean "not." Sort the words below into the correct box. Then, select from the words in the first box to complete the sentences below.

Word Bank			
distribute	dispenser	disturbance	disqualified
dilapidated	digest	disruption	disreputable
dissimilar	dissatisfied	dishonorable	

Prefix means "apart, in different directions"	Prefix means "not"

❶ We should not do any heavy exercise after eating a large meal since we need time to

_____ our food.

❷ The police boarded up the old _____ building to prevent children from playing inside.

❸ We need to _____ these flyers to all students in the school.

❹ When Mary took her little lamb to school one day, which was against the rules, she created

quite a _____.

Name: _____   Date: _____

Read and Reason:
Prefixes *di-*, *dif-*, and *dis-*

Directions: Read the passages. Circle the words with the prefixes *di-*, *dif-*, and *dis-*. Then, answer the questions on page 163.

Passage A

Rocks or Brownies?

"Oh no!" cried Janice. She had tried to bake brownies, but she had difficulty figuring out the correct amounts of ingredients. She had been distracted as she baked, creating quite a mess. By the end of her efforts, her hair was in disarray and the kitchen was in a state of disorder. The bake sale was due to start in an hour, but Janice's brownies were totally dissatisfactory!

"These are NOT brownies!" she told herself firmly as she clunked the little rocks onto the counter. "People won't be able to digest these things. After biting into one of these disgusting concoctions, people will dismiss me as a disreputable baker! Some people might even experience discomfort when these stones sink into their tummy! From now on, I will keep my distance from baking. But, thank goodness! There is a Quick Shop by the school, and I have just enough time to buy some baked goods to take!"

Read and Reason:
Prefixes *di-*, *dif-*, and *dis-* (cont.)

Passage B

Cultural Diversity

Most anthropologists believe that the first human beings lived in Africa, long, long ago. Since then, groups of people have been distributed throughout the world, successfully adapting to widely differing conditions. These separate and distinct societies differed markedly from one another. Many of these dissimilarities persist to this day. This variety in human societies or cultures is called *cultural diversity*.

Different cultural groups can be identified along many discrete dimensions: time and place, dress, traditions, race, ethnicity, and language, to name a few. Other aspects of culture may be less easy to distinguish. For example, cultural groups may differ in how their societies are organized, how they think about morality, and how they interact with their environment.

Cultural diversity is difficult to quantify. Some scientists believe that the number of languages spoken in a region is a good indication of diversity. According to this measure, the world's cultural diversity may be disappearing. Research carried out in the 1990s showed that, on average, one language fell into disuse every two weeks.

The United Nations Educational, Scientific, and Cultural Organization (UNESCO) attempts to protect cultural diversity. Its Universal Declaration on Cultural Diversity, adopted in 2001, is the first international effort to preserve and promote cultural diversity and intercultural exchange.

Scientists argue that biodiversity, the variety in all forms of life, is essential to the long-term survival of life on Earth. Likewise, cultural diversity may be vital for the long-term survival of humanity. In fact, UNESCO recognizes cultural diversity as the "common heritage of humanity" and "as necessary for humankind as biodiversity is for nature."

Read and Reason:
Prefixes *di-*, *dif-*, and *dis-* (cont.)

Directions: Read Passage A and respond to the questions below.

❶ Select three words from the passage: one beginning with the prefix *di-*, one with *dis-*, and the other with *dif-*.

_____

_____

_____

❷ Of the *di-*, *dis-*, and *dif-* words in the passage, tell which one means:

a. "not" satisfactory: _____

b. "not" having a good reputation: _____

c. unable to concentrate because of attention being pulled "apart, in different directions":

_____

❸ Select any *di- dis-*, or *dif-* word from the passage and use it in your own sentence.

_____

_____

_____

. . . .

Directions: Read Passage B and respond to the questions below.

❶ Think of a person you know. List all the ways in which you are different from this person. Then circle the differences that could be cultural.

_____

_____

_____

_____

❷ Why might the number of languages spoken in an area be a good indication of cultural diversity?

_____

_____

_____

❸ List three words from the passage that contain the *di-*, *dif-*, and *dis-* prefix. For each, tell how the meaning reflects "apart," "in different directions," or "not."

_____

_____

_____

Prefixes *a-*, *ab-*, and *abs-*

Standards: Uses word origins and derivations to understand word meaning (McREL 2.0)
Uses a variety of sentence structures to expand and embed ideas (McREL 2.3)
Uses conventions of spelling in written compositions (McREL 3.9)
Uses basic elements of structural analysis to decode unknown words (McREL 4.0)
Draws conclusions and makes inferences based on explicit and implicit information in texts (McREL 7.5)

Materials

- *Divide and Conquer: Prefixes a-, ab-, and abs-* (page 167)

- *Combine and Create: Prefixes a-, ab-, and abs-* (page 168)

- *Read and Reason: Prefixes a-, ab-, and abs-* (pages 169–171)

Teaching Tips

- This lesson presents the directional prefixes *a-*, *ab-*, and *abs-*, meaning "away, from, away from."

- These prefixes appear in words that students may already know but have never associated with the idea of "away, from." For example, *absent* students are "away from" class; to *abduct* means to kidnap and lead "away;" *abnormal* behavior is "away from" the norm. All *a-*, *ab-*, and *abs-* words contain the idea of separation or distance.

- These prefixes describe the literal and physical idea of "away, from": a paper towel *absorbs* spilled water by soaking it "away from" the surface; we *avert* our eyes from a scary movie scene by physically "turning" them "away from" the screen; when we scrape skin "away from" our knees.

Teaching Tips *(cont.)*

- The prefix also describes the figurative idea of "away, from": *abnormal* behavior is unusual because it is "away from" the norm or standard; in *abstract* art, a painter "draws" an image "away from" the concrete object; an *avocation* is a hobby that, figuratively, takes us "away from" our regular work or vocation; a ruler who *abdicates* the throne declares that he or she is moving "away from" power.

- Many words beginning with these prefixes can be both literal and figurative: a sponge *absorbs* water (literal), but a good student *absorbs* the lesson (figurative); an *abrupt* cliff is physically steep (literal), but *abrupt* manners are curt and "broken off" (figurative); kitchen cleansers can be *abrasive* and literally scrape coatings "from" the surface, but comments can also be harsh and *abrasive* (figurative).

- These prefixes appear in many academic words that express the figurative, rather than literal, idea of "away, from": *abstention, abrasive, abrupt, aberrant, absolute.*

Guided Practice

Activate Background Knowledge

1. Write the word *absent* on the board, and draw a slash after the letter *s* (*abs/ent*). Tell students that the base *–ent* means "being, are." Ask, "Where are the *absent* students? Are they here or are they *away*?" When students answer "away," draw a circle around the prefix *abs-* and explain that it means "away, from, away from."

Prefixes *a-*, *ab-*, and *abs-* (cont.)

Guided Practice (cont.) ·············

2. Write the word *abduct*, and draw a slash after the letter *b* (*ab/duct*). Say, "When we are at playgrounds, we need to be alert in case some stranger may want to kidnap or *abduct* us." Ask, "Who can tell me what *abduct* means, using the word 'away'?" (to lead or take a person away from a place) Write the word *avert* on the board and say, "Pretend you are watching a horror movie and you want to turn your eyes 'away from' the screen: you could either cover your face with your hands or turn your head 'away from' the screen and *avert* your eyes." Explain that the prefix meaning "away, from, away from" has three possible forms: *a-* as in *avert*, *ab-* as in *abduct*, and *abs-* as in *absent*.

3. Ask students, "When I fall on the sidewalk and scrape skin 'away from' my knee, what word beginning with *ab-* describes the scrapes?" (*abrasion[s]*)

Divide and Conquer

4. Distribute copies of the *Divide and Conquer: Prefixes a-, ab-, and abs-* activity sheet (page 167) to students. Guide students through the activity. The practice sheet may be duplicated for each student and/or projected on a projector. Starting with the first word, *absorb*, ask, "If the base *sorb-* means to 'soak' and the prefix *ab-* means 'away, from,' then *absorb* means to 'soak away from.' Which definition in the Answer Bank has this meaning?" (The answer is F; to soak up.)

5. Repeat step 4 with the word *abscond*. Tell students, "If the base *cond* means 'hide' and the prefix *abs-* means 'away, from,' then *abscond* means to 'hide away.' Which definition in the Answer Bank has this meaning?" (The answer is C; to flee quickly and in secret [usually with stolen goods].) Select a few more words from the list and repeat the process.

Combine and Create

6. Distribute copies of the *Combine and Create: Prefixes a-, ab-, and abs-* activity sheet (page 168) to students. Ask students to work individually or in pairs to complete the words with the correct form of the prefix: *a-*, *ab-*, or *abs-*. Upon completion, ask students to read their answers aloud, making sure that they read the definitions. Ask them to explain how each word means "away, from, away from."

Prefixes *a-*, *ab-*, and *abs-* *(cont.)*

Guided Practice *(cont.)* ·············

Read and Reason

7. Distribute copies of the *Read and Reason: Prefixes a-, ab-, and abs-* activity sheets (pages 169–171) to students. Have students read one or both passages and answer the questions. If the passages are too difficult for independent reading, ask students to read in pairs or follow along as you read aloud. Tell them to raise their hands when they hear a word with the prefixes *a-*, *ab-*, or *abs-*. Students should circle the words they identify. After you have finished reading, return to the circled words and ask volunteers to explain what they mean. Then, invite students to answer the questions.

: **Extend and Explore**
: Choose from among the
: activities located on the Teacher
: Resource CD to give students
: extra practice with the prefixes
: *a-*, *ab-*, and *abs-*.

Answer Key ·····················

Divide and Conquer: Prefixes *a-*, *ab-*, and *abs-* (page 167)

1. absorb: away, from, away from; soak; F
2. avert: away, from, away from; turn; I
3. abrupt: away, from, away from; break; J
4. abnormal: away, from, away from; norm, usual; H
5. abscond: away, from, away from; hide; C
6. abstain: away, from, away from; hold, keep; B
7. abduct: away, from, away from; lead; A
8. abstract: away, from, away from; pull, draw, drag; G
9. avocation: away, from, away from; call, voice; D
10. abrasive: away, from, away from; scrape; E

Combine and Create: Prefixes *a-*, *ab-*, and *abs-* (page 168)

1. avert
2. abnormal
3. absenteeism
4. abstract
5. abrupt
6. abstention
7. abdicated
8. aberration
9. absolved
10. abhor

Read and Reason: Prefixes *a-*, *ab-*, and *abs-* (pages 169–171)

Passage A: *avert, abduct, abdicate, abhor, aberrations, abnormal, abscond, abrasion, absolve*

1. Answers will vary. See list above.
2. No; there is no base word.
3. Answers will vary.

Passage B: *abruptly, abdicated, abnormal, aberrant, absent, absolutely, abhorred, abused, avert, abstain, absorption, absolve, abhorrent, abdication, abrogation, abandoned*

Answers to questions 1, 2, and 3 will vary. For Question 3, accept responses which express the idea of separation, removal, distance, etc.

Name: _____   Date: _____

Divide and Conquer:
Prefixes *a-*, *ab-*, and *abs-*

Directions: Break apart each word below. Write the prefix and its meaning in the first column after the word. In the next column, the base and its meaning are provided. Combine the meanings of the prefix and base and select a definition from the Answer Bank. An example has been done for you.

Answer Bank
A. to kidnap
B. to refrain from voting; to keep away from an activity
C. to flee quickly and in secret (usually with stolen goods)
D. a hobby, pastime, diversion that you do when away from work
E. harsh; irritating, scraping
F. to soak up
G. vague; theoretical; not concrete
H. irregular, unusual, veering from the norm
I. to turn away; to prevent from happening
J. sudden, unexpected; also, steep

word	prefix means	base means	definition
❶ absorb	ab- = away, from, away from	sorb- = soak	F
❷ avert		vert- = turn	
❸ abrupt		rupt- = break	
❹ abnormal		norm- = norm, usual	
❺ abscond		cond- = hide	
❻ abstain		tain- = hold, keep	
❼ abduct		duct- = lead	
❽ abstract		tract- = pull, draw, drag	
❾ avocation		voc- = call, voice	
❿ abrasive		ras- = scrape	

Name: _____   Date: _____

Combine and Create:
Prefixes *a-*, *ab-*, and *abs-*

Directions: Attach the correct form of the prefixes (*a-*, *ab-*, or *abs-*) to these bases to generate the academic word described in each sentence.

Academic Word	Sentence
1 _____ vert	I cannot bear to watch. I will turn my eyes "away from" the sight!
2 _____ normal	Your behavior has been strange and "away from" the norm lately!
3 _____ enteeism	A lot of students have been "away from" class these last few weeks!
4 _____ tract	The explanation in the textbook was vague and hard to follow. It was "away from" being clear and concrete.
5 _____ rupt	The car came to a sudden halt, braking to a speed of zero "away from" 30 mph in an instant.
6 _____ tention	We have only three yes votes and four no votes. Fifteen people refused to mark their ballots and stayed "away from" voting.
7 _____ dicated	The king declared that he would step down from the throne in order to marry a commoner. He was stepping "away from" his position of power.
8 _____ erration	It was out of character for you to do such a thing! Your behavior was unusual and far "away from" your regular conduct.
9 _____ solved	The courts freed him from all charges, declaring him freed "from" responsibility for the alleged crime.
10 _____ hor	I shudder at the thought of spending more time with him! I will keep "away from" him out of fear and disgust!

Name: _____   Date: _____

Read and Reason:
Prefixes *a-*, *ab-*, and *abs-*

Directions: Read the passages. Circle the words with the prefixes *a-*, *ab-*, and *abs-*. Then, answer the questions on page 171.

Passage A

News Flash

Today in Courtsville, police were able to avert a tragedy when three masked men tried to abduct the queen! According to the spokesman for their group, the trio's goal was to force her to abdicate the throne. "We abhor her policies," he said. "Her decisions don't make sense—they are aberrations. And we think she is too old. It is abnormal for anyone to live this long!" One man was briefly able to abscond with the royal crown. But he was caught, and the crown was recovered. Her Majesty escaped with only a small abrasion on her elbow where it scraped against the rough vest of her captor. Surprisingly, the queen announced her intention to absolve her captors of all guilt for their crimes. They may go free as early as tomorrow.

Read and Reason:
Prefixes *a-*, *ab-*, and *abs-* (cont.)

Passage B

The Woman I Love

"I have found it impossible to carry the heavy burden of responsibility and to discharge my duties as King as I would wish to do, without the help and support of the woman I love." With these words, uttered abruptly in December 1936, King Edward VIII of the United Kingdom abdicated his throne.

By the time Wallis Simpson met the future king, she was estranged from her second husband. In 1934, she became Edward's mistress. Two years later, after Edward took the throne as King, Wallis divorced her second husband and Edward proposed marriage to her. Most people in that time period looked on a twice-divorced woman as abnormal and as exhibiting aberrant behavior.

Even before the marriage proposal, their relationship was controversial. When Edward first introduced Wallis to his mother and father, who were the king and queen of England, he caused a stir because divorced people were generally excluded from court. Such individuals were expected to absent themselves from formal family gatherings because the royal family absolutely abhorred scandal. Edward also abused protocol by watching the proclamation of his accession to the throne from a palace window in the company of Wallis, who was still married at the time. Many onlookers tried to avert their eyes from the scandalous sight, saying that Edward should abstain from associating with a divorced woman. Edward's absorption with Wallis began to interfere with his official duties.

The king's desire to marry a woman who had two living ex-husbands caused a constitutional crisis. As monarch, the king was supreme governor of the Church of England. The Church did not permit divorced people, whose ex-spouses were still alive, to marry. Constitutionally, the king was required to follow the Church's teachings, so his proposed marriage caused a conflict. Neither the government nor the Church could absolve Edward from his blatant abuse of British laws and customs. Furthermore, many government officials found Wallis abhorrent—politically, socially, and morally unsuitable as a prospective consort to the king.

The king wanted to marry Wallis and keep the throne, but government officials rejected his ideas and threatened to resign if the king married her. Eventually, the king decided he had no option but to abdicate. The abdication ended several years of gossip, debate, and royal intrigue. But questions still surround Edward's abrogation of his responsibility to rule. Was he so much in love that he foolishly believed he could maintain his power and still marry Wallis? What would the public have thought if he abandoned Wallis to keep the throne? Is his story a saga of British royalty or simply a love story?

Read and Reason:
Prefixes *a-*, *ab-*, and *abs-* (cont.)

Directions: Read Passage A and respond to the questions below.

❶ List the words in the passage that begin with the prefixes *a-*, *ab-*, and *abs-*.

_____

_____

_____

❷ Does the word *able* belong on the list? How can you tell?

_____

_____

_____

❸ Define the word *absolve* in your own words. Be sure to use "away from" in your definition.

_____

_____

_____

. . . .

Directions: Read Passage B and respond to the questions below.

❶ Do you think King Edward should have abdicated? Why or why not?

_____

_____

_____

❷ Do you think the British government should have interfered with the king's personal relationships? Why or why not?

_____

_____

_____

❸ Explain how the following words mean "away, from, away from": *abdicate*, *abhor*, *abandon*, and *absolve*.

_____

_____

_____

_____

Prefixes *super-* and *sur-*

Standards: Uses word origins and derivations to understand word meaning (McREL 2.0)
Uses a variety of sentence structures to expand and embed ideas (McREL 2.3)
Uses conventions of spelling in written compositions (McREL 3.9)
Uses basic elements of structural analysis to decode unknown words (McREL 4.0)
Draws conclusions and makes inferences based on explicit and implicit information in texts (McREL 7.5)

Materials

- *Divide and Conquer: Prefixes super- and sur-* (page 175)

- *Combine and Create: Prefixes super- and sur-* (page 176)

- *Read and Reason: Prefixes super- and sur-* (pages 177–179)

Teaching Tips

- This lesson presents the directional prefix *super-* and its variant form (from French) *sur-* meaning "on top of, over, above."

- Most students will readily recognize the prefix *super-* from such everyday words as *Superman, supermarket, super-duper,* and *supersize.*

- The prefixes *super-* and *sur-* describe things that are physically and literally "over, above" other things. On a map of North America, Lake *Superior* is "over, on top of" the other Great Lakes to the south (it is also *superior* in size, being the largest freshwater lake in the world); when we *superimpose* a plate over a bowl, we literally place the plate "on top of" the bowl; a *surveyor* uses a tripod to stand physically "over" the terrain to be *surveyed* and measured; the *surface* of a table is the "top" portion.

Teaching Tips *(cont.)*

- The prefix also describes things and people that are "over, above" others in rank, position, or importance: a *superior* officer is figuratively "over" lower-ranking officers; a district *superintendent* is a high-ranking official who "oversees" the operations of several schools; a *supermarket* is larger and sells more items than a regular market; a *supervisor* "oversees" other workers; when we *surmount* obstacles in life, we "overcome" them; when we *surrender* in battle, we turn ourselves "over" to the victor.

- The prefix *sur-* also describes things that are added "on top of" existing things: a fuel *surcharge* is an additional fee placed "on top of" the regular charge for services; a *surplus* is an amount that is left "over"; a *surtax* is "an additional tax."

- These prefixes do not assimilate.

Guided Practice

Activate Background Knowledge

1. Ask students about *Superman:* "What one thing does *Superman* do that we cannot do?" (he flies) Write the word *Superman* on the board, writing a slash after the letter *r* (*Super/man*). Tell students, "*Superman's* ability to fly over the world is indicated by the prefix *super-,* which means 'above, over, on top of.'"

Prefixes *super-* and *sur-* (cont.)

Guided Practice (cont.) · · · · · · · · · · · ·

2. Build on this explanation, moving from the literal "over" to the figurative "above, over." Say, "Because *Superman* can fly 'over' our heads, he is also able to do many other *super* things, such as stop speeding trains, blow out a forest fire, and pull out trees by their roots." Explain that when we say *super*, we mean not only things that are physically "above" us, but also things that are "up there" at a high level of performance. Explain that many famous people are stars, and that a few of them are *superstars*. Discuss *superstar*, explaining that a *superstar* has a higher status "over, above" regular stars.

3. Tell students to work in pairs or teams to brainstorm some *super-* words. Encourage them to be creative, and accept their answers. Have them write some of their favorite *super-* words on the board and discuss them.

4. Write the form *sur-* on the board, explaining that many words beginning with this form of the prefix also describe things that are "over, on top of, above" things. Point out the *surface* of the desk, showing that it is "on top of" the rest of the desk. Pretend to stand on your toes as you look "over" the room, taking a *survey* (a survey is an "over-view"). Now ask if anyone knows what a *surplus* is (things that are left over). Point out the word *over* in their explanation and remind them that *super-* and *sur-* are prefixes meaning "over, above, on top of."

Divide and Conquer

5. Distribute copies of the *Divide and Conquer: Prefixes super- and sur-* activity sheet (page 175) to students. Guide students through the activity. The practice sheet may be duplicated for each student and/or projected on a projector. Start with the first word, *supervise*, and say, "If the base *vis-* means to 'see, look' and the prefix *super-* means 'above, over, on top of,' then *supervise* means to 'over-see' or 'to look over others.' Which definition in the Answer Bank has this meaning?" (The answer is J; to oversee or manage.)

6. Repeat step 5 with the word *superficial*, which may be new to some students. Tell students, "If the base *fic-* means 'face' and the prefix *super-* means 'above, over, on top of,' then *superficial* means 'over the face or surface; on top of the face of things.' What answer in the Answer Bank expresses this meaning?" (The answer is F; occurring only on the surface; not deep or profound.) Pick a few more words from the list and repeat the process.

Combine and Create

7. Distribute copies of the *Combine and Create: Prefixes super- and sur-* activity sheet (page 176) to students. Ask students to work individually or in pairs to complete the sentences with the prefixes *super-* and *sur-*. Then ask students to read the sentences aloud. Discuss the direction of "over, above, on top of" in each word.

Prefixes *super-* and *sur-* *(cont.)*

Guided Practice *(cont.)* · · · · · · · · · · · ·

Read and Reason

8. Distribute copies of the *Read and Reason: Prefixes super- and sur-* activity sheets (pages 177–179) to students. Have students read one or both passages and answer the questions. If the passages are too difficult for independent reading, ask students to read in pairs or follow along as you read aloud. Tell them to raise their hands when they hear a word with the prefixes *super-* or *sur-*. Students should circle the words they identify. After you have finished reading, return to the circled words and ask volunteers to explain what they mean. Then, invite students to answer the questions.

> **Extend and Explore**
> Choose from among the activities located on the Teacher Resource CD to give students extra practice with the prefixes *super-* and *sur-*.

Answer Key ·

Divide and Conquer: Prefixes *super-* and *sur-* (page 175)

1. supervise: above, over, on top of; see, look; J
2. superior: above, over, on top of; more; I
3. surcharge: above, over, on top of; charge; E
4. surrender: above, over, on top of; give; B
5. surveyor: above, over, on top of; see, view; C
6. surmount: above, over, on top of; mount, climb; A
7. superfluous: above, over, on top of; flow; H
8. superficial: above, over, on top of; face; F
9. surtax: above, over, on top of; tax; G
10. superb: above, over, on top of; no base; D

Combine and Create: Prefixes *super-* and *sur-* (page 176)

1. superlative
2. surpassed
3. surveillance
4. superpower
5. surplus
6. superfluous
7. superintendent
8. surface

Read and Reason: Prefixes *super-* and *sur-* (pages 177–179)

Passage A = *surveillance, surveyed, supervisor, superior, super-cheapskate, surpassed, surplus, surprise, super-vigilant, superb*

1. Answers will vary. See list above.
2a. surprise
2b. surveillance
2c. surplus
3. superior or superb

Passage B = *Superman, superhero, surpasses, surround, superb, surmised, super-speed, superhuman, surmount, supersensitive, surface, survive, superlative, surrender, superbly, superior*

1. Answers will vary.
2. Answers will vary.
3. Answers will vary, but accept responses expressing the idea of "high," "over," "rising," "top," etc.

Name: _____   Date: _____

Divide and Conquer: Prefixes *super-* and *sur-*

Directions: Break apart each word below. Write the prefix and its meaning in the first column after the word. In the next column, the base and its meaning are provided. Combine the meanings of the prefix and base and select a definition from the Answer Bank. An example has been done for you.

Answer Bank
A. overcome (obstacles or difficulties)
B. to hand over to a victor
C. one who measures and inspects tracts of land
D. outstanding in quality; excellent
E. an additional fee imposed on top of a regular charge
F. occurring only on the surface; not deep or profound
G. an additional tax
H. unnecessary and left over; excessive
I. higher in rank or importance; better
J. to oversee or manage

word	prefix means	base means	definition
❶ supervise	super- = above, over, on top of	vis- = see, look	J
❷ superior		-ior = more	
❸ surcharge		charge = charge	
❹ surrender		rend- = give	
❺ surveyor		vey- = see, view	
❻ surmount		mount- = mount, climb	
❼ superfluous		flu- = flow	
❽ superficial		fic- = face	
❾ surtax		tax = tax	
❿ superb		no base	

Name: _____   Date: _____

Combine and Create:
Prefixes *super-* and *sur-*

Directions: The words in the Word Bank begin with prefixes *super-* and *sur-*. Complete the sentences below by writing the most appropriate word in the blank.

Word Bank			
superlative	surplus	surveillance	surpassed
superpower	superfluous	surface	superintendent

❶ In the sequence "good, better, best," "better" is the comparative degree, and "best" is the _____ degree.

❷ "What a fantastic meal that was! You have _____ yourself!"

❸ The police placed the suspect under round-the-clock _____ and never took their eyes off him.

❹ What do you think makes the United States of America a world _____ ?

❺ After the garage sale, we gave all the _____ merchandise to the thrift store.

❻ This cake is so sweet that it would be _____ to add sugar to the icing.

❼ Ms. Gonzalez decided to step down after serving for 15 years as the _____ of the school district.

❽ My teacher wipes down the _____ of her desk every Friday afternoon.

Name: _____   Date: _____

Read and Reason:
Prefixes *super-* and *sur-*

Directions: Read the passages. Circle the words with the prefixes *super-* and *sur-*. Then, answer the questions on page 179.

Passage A

Josh Is Not Joshing: Being Frank About Frank

Josh sat watching the surveillance video at the bank. He was the night guard. His job was to keep his eyes on the camera. Every two hours, he also surveyed the premises by walking around the property. His supervisor, Frank, checked up on him every so often. Frank was Josh's superior at the bank. Although Frank's salary was higher, he was a super-cheapskate! No one surpassed him when it came to pinching pennies! Josh could always tell when Frank was coming for a spot-check.

He could hear the cheap, clunky army surplus boots that Frank always wore. Frank loved to buy those ugly, leftover things! That is why Frank could never surprise Josh. Luckily, the spot-checks were not necessary. Josh was a super-vigilant watchman and a superb employee.

Read and Reason:
Prefixes *super-* and *sur-* (cont.)

Passage B

Faster Than a Speeding Bullet

Superman is a fictional comic book superhero. His character first appeared in a 1938 comic book and since then has been featured in newspaper comic strips, radio serials, television shows, movies, and video games. Superman's appearance is distinctive and iconic: a blue, red, and yellow costume, a cape, and a stylized S shield on his chest. Because he clearly surpasses all human beings in strength, he is sometimes called the "Man of Steel."

Legends that surround Superman have become more elaborate over the years. According to these legends, he was born on the planet Krypton. His scientist father sent him to Earth in a rocket just before his home planet was destroyed. A Kansas farm family discovered the baby, who was raised as Clark Kent. Clark is shy, polite, and embodies superb Midwestern values.

His Earth parents never surmised their son's gifts. Yet Superman started displaying superhuman abilities as a young boy. These grew stronger as he matured. The adult Superman is "faster than a speeding bullet, more powerful than a locomotive, and able to leap tall buildings in a single bound." He can surmount skyscrapers with a single stride. He also has super-speed and superhuman strength. He can fly and has X-ray vision and supersensitive hearing.

Superman is invulnerable to most attacks unless he encounters Kryptonite, radioactive mineral debris from the surface of his home planet. Exposure to Kryptonite nullifies Superman's powers and immobilizes him with pain. Lead blocks the radiation so that Superman can survive.

Superman is a hero in the mythic tradition of Hercules. He fights for social justice and against tyranny. In ancient Greek mythology, Hercules possessed superlative powers over monsters and demons. But in the 1930s and 1940s, villains in Superman comics were often crooked businessmen and politicians, whom audiences during the Great Depression and New Deal viewed as dangerous monsters! Although Superman's villains all fight firecely, they all eventually surrender to the Man of Steel, who overcomes them in superbly impressive ways because he is morally and physically superior to them.

Read and Reason:
Prefixes *super-* and *sur-* (cont.)

Directions: Read Passage A and respond to the questions below.

1 List two words from the passage that begin with the prefix *sur-* and two words that begin with the prefix *super-* (you may include hyphenated words).

_____

_____

_____

_____

2 Of the words in the passage, tell which one means:

a. to "over-" take and startle someone unexpectedly: _____

b. an "over-" view and scanning an area: _____

c. one or more items that are left "over" and excessive: _____

3 Which *super-* word in the passage means "outstanding, excellent"?

_____

. . . .

Directions: Read Passage B and respond to the questions below.

1 Select three of Superman's "super powers." For each, tell how it might help him fight crime.

_____

_____

_____

2 Superman's character has been part of popular media for almost 75 years. Why do you think people continue to enjoy him?

_____

_____

_____

_____

3 Explain how the words *superior, surpass, surmount,* and *superb* mean "over, above."

_____

_____

_____

_____

Prefix *ad-* and Its Assimilated Forms

Standards: Uses word origins and derivations to understand word meaning (McREL 2.0)
Uses a variety of sentence structures to expand and embed ideas (McREL 2.3)
Uses conventions of spelling in written compositions (McREL 3.9)
Uses basic elements of structural analysis to decode unknown words (McREL 4.0)
Draws conclusions and makes inferences based on explicit and implicit information in texts (McREL 7.5)

Materials

- *Divide and Conquer: Prefix ad- and Its Assimilated Forms* (page 184)

- *Combine and Create: Prefix ad- and Its Assimilated Forms* (page 185)

- *Read and Reason: Prefix ad- and Its Assimilated Forms* (pages 186–188)

Teaching Tips

- This lesson presents the prefix *ad-* and its assimilated forms meaning "to, toward, add to."

- Students already know many words beginning with this prefix, but they may not have thought about them as having the directional force of "to, toward, add to." Sample words include *adhere* (to "stick, cling" to a surface), *adjacent* ("lying" or "situated next to something"), and *addition* (the "adding of one number to another").

- This prefix undergoes a very high rate of assimilation, appearing in many words from everyday vocabulary (e.g., *affect, appreciate, applause*), academic vocabulary (e.g., *alleviate, abbreviate*), and content-area vocabulary (e.g., *adjective, alliteration*).

Teaching Tips *(cont.)*

- *Spelling Hint*: Nearly all English words containing a doubled consonant after an initial *a-* contain the assimilated prefix *ad-*.

- This prefix appears in words with the literal, physical meaning of "to, toward": a magnet *attracts* metals that it physically pulls "toward" itself; tape or glue *adheres* to paper by literally sticking "to" it.

- Many *ad-* words express the figurative idea of "to, toward, add to": we are drawn "to" *attractive* people or ideas without moving physically in their direction; we *adhere* to rules when we stick "to" them without literally clinging to anything.

- Many *ad-* words describe "adding to" something and making it "more." When we *accelerate*, we "add to" our speed. Even the word *assimilation*, which students learn as they study prefixes, contains *assimilated ad-*: when we "add" certain consonants "to" each other, we often need to *assimilate* them and make the one consonant "similar" "to" the other.

Guided Practice

Activate Background Knowledge

1. Show students a tape dispenser. Stick a piece of the tape to a surface and tell students, "The name Scotch® Tape is a brand name for Scotch-Brand Adhesive Tape. Why do you think this is called *adhesive* tape?" Write the word *adhesive* on the board, circling the prefix *ad-*. Explain, "If the base of this word, *hes-*, means 'stick, cling,' what does the prefix *ad-* mean?" (to). Now elicit other forms of the word: *adhesive* tape has powers of *adhesion*. It *adheres* to things. The prefix *ad-* means, "to, toward, add to."

Prefix *ad-* and Its Assimilated Forms *(cont.)*

Guided Practice *(cont.)* ·············

2. Explain that we also use the word *adhere* when we "stick to" the rules or directions; people *adhere* to a diet when they "stick to" it. The prefix *ad-* means "to, toward, add to" in both a literal sense and in a figurative sense.

3. Point out that nearly all words in English that begin with *a-* followed by a doubled consonant are *ad-* words. Explain that the *d* of *ad-* often changes into the consonant of the very next letter. This is called *assimilation*. Tell students that whenever they encounter a word beginning with *a-* followed by a doubled consonant, they should divide and conquer between the doubled consonant and translate the prefix as *ad-* = "to, toward, add to."

4. If you have a magnet, demonstrate that it attracts metals. Write the word *attract* on the board. Tell students that this word was originally *adtract*. But because it is hard to pronounce, we spell it as *attract*. Ask students to use the word *to* or *toward* in their explanation of magnetic attraction. Now ask them if we can use the words *attraction* and *attractive* in a figurative sense. We see previews of coming *attractions*, which draw us "to" the movies.

Divide and Conquer

5. Distribute copies of the *Divide and Conquer: Prefix ad- and Its Assimilated Forms* activity sheet (page 184) to students. Guide students through the activity. The practice sheet may be duplicated for each student and/or projected on a projector. Explain that every word in this list begins with the prefix *ad-*, meaning "to, toward, add to," but that some words have the assimilated *ad-*, resulting in a doubled consonant after the *a-*.

6. Advise students when they divide and conquer to divide after the letter *d* or between the doubled consonant. Starting with the first word, *attract*, ask, "If the base *tract-* means to 'pull, draw, drag' and the prefix *ad-* means 'to, toward, add to' (but we assimilate *ad-* to *at-* to produce a doubled consonant and make the word easier to pronounce), then *attract* means 'to draw or pull something to something.' Which definition in the Answer Bank has this meaning?" (The answer is E; to draw to oneself; to entice.)

7. Repeat step 6 with the word *adjective*. Explain, "If the base *ject-* means 'throw, cast' and the prefix *ad-* means 'to, toward, add to,' then an *adjective* is a word we 'throw or cast to or toward another word.' Which definition in the Answer Bank has this meaning?" (The answer is B; a word added to a noun to modify it.) Point out that in this word the prefix *ad-* remains unchanged because we can easily pronounce the consonant cluster *dj*. Select a few more words from the list and repeat the process.

Prefix *ad-* and Its Assimilated Forms _(cont.)

Guided Practice *(cont.)* ·············

Combine and Create

8. Distribute copies of the *Combine and Create: Prefix ad- and Its Assimilated Forms* activity sheet (page 185) to students. Ask students to work individually or in pairs to complete the academic words. Present the first word by writing on the board: *ad + literation*. Say, "This word means that we 'add' 'letters' to one another in succession, as in 'Peter Piper picked a peck of pickled peppers.' But in English, we do not say *adliteration* because the combination *dl* is hard to pronounce. So, we change the *d* into the next consonant, resulting in two *l*'s." At the end of the activity, have students report their answers and explain how they changed the prefix *ad-* into its assimilated forms.

Read and Reason

9. Distribute copies of the *Read and Reason: Prefix ad- and Its Assimilated Forms* activity sheets (pages 186–188) to students. Have students read one or both passages and answer the questions. If the passages are too difficult for independent reading, ask students to read in pairs or follow along as you read aloud. Tell them to raise their hands when they hear a word that contains the prefix *ad-* or its assimilated forms (*a* followed by a doubled consonant). Students should circle the words they identify. After you have finished reading, return to each of the circled words and ask volunteers to explain what they mean. Then, invite students to answer the questions.

> **Extend and Explore**
> Choose from among the activities located on the Teacher Resource CD to give students extra practice with the prefix *ad-*, including its assimilated forms.

Prefix *ad-* and Its Assimilated Forms *(cont.)*

Answer Key ·······················

Divide and Conquer: Prefix *ad-* and Its Assimilated Forms (page 184)

1. attract: to, toward, add to; pull, draw, drag; E
2. adhere: to, toward, add to; stick, cling; J
3. appreciate: to, toward, add to; value, price; G
4. abbreviate: to, toward, add to; short; F
5. affect: to, toward, add to; do, make; D
6. accelerate: to, toward, add to; fast, swift; C
7. addition: to, toward, add to; give; I
8. adjective: to, toward, add to; throw, cast; B
9. admonish: to, toward, add to; warn; A
10. advent: to, toward, add to; come, go; H

Combine and Create: Prefix *ad-* and Its Assimilated Forms (page 185)

1. alliteration
2. assimilation
3. attraction
4. apparition
5. accusation
6. aggression
7. abbreviation
8. acceleration
9. aggravation
10. appreciation

Read and Reason: Prefix *ad-* and Its Assimilated Forms (pages 186–188)

Passage A: *adhesive, appealing, attached, adhered, advertise, aggressive, ads (for advertisements), attracted, abbreviation, apply*

1. Answers will vary.
2a. Answers will vary. Accept responses expressing the idea of drawing objects or people "to, toward" someone or something. Attractive people draw others *toward* them, magnets attract metals by drawing them *toward* themselves, etc.

2b. Answers will vary. Accept responses expressing the idea of "adding to" or directing oneself "to, toward" something else. When we apply tape, we *add* it to the paper; when we apply for a job, we send our request *to* the employer.
2c. Answers will vary. Accept responses expressing the idea of turning people's attention toward a product. We turn our heads toward an advertising sign, or an ad might drive us into considering a new purchase, etc.
3. Answers will vary.

Passage B: *advice, appears, admired, address, addiction, adversarial, adoption, advocating, adult, additional, adolescents, admiration, affirms, admonishes, adhere, admits, adequate*

1. Answers will vary.
2. Answers will vary.
3. Answers will vary. Accept responses expressing the idea of moving or directing our attention *toward* a person or thing. We look up to people when we address them, we send mail to an address, etc.

Identify the Prefix and Pick the Best Word (page 189)

1. c
2. b
3. d
4. c
5. b
6. a
7. a

Divide and Conquer:
Prefix *ad-* and Its Assimilated Forms

Directions: Break apart each word below. Write the prefix and its meaning in the first column after the word. In the next column, the base and its meaning are provided. Combine the meanings of the prefix and base and select a definition from the Answer Bank. An example has been done for you.

Answer Bank
A. to chastise or reprove gently; to give a warning to
B. a word added to a noun to modify it
C. to speed up
D. to influence; to make an impression on
E. to draw toward oneself; to entice
F. to write in shortened form
G. to value or esteem; to consider of high value
H. arrival; also, the 40 days preceding Christmas
I. the operation of combining numbers to increase their sum
J. to cling to; to follow (directions) closely

word	prefix means	base means	definition
❶ attract	ad- = to, toward, add to	tract- = pull, draw, drag	E
❷ adhere		her- = stick, cling	
❸ appreciate		preci- = value, price	
❹ abbreviate		brev- = short	
❺ affect		fect- = do, make	
❻ accelerate		celer- = fast, swift	
❼ addition		dit- = give	
❽ adjective		ject- = throw, cast	
❾ admonish		mon- = warn	
❿ advent		vent- = come, go	

Name: _____   Date: _____

Combine and Create:
Prefix *ad-* and Its Assimilated Forms

Directions: Complete each academic word to fit the sentence below. Every word will begin with the prefix *ad-*, but you must change the letter *d* of the prefix to match the next consonant in the word. In every word, the result will be a doubled consonant.

Academic Word	Sentence
❶ _____ literation	Peter Piper picked a peck of pickled peppers.
❷ _____ similation	Many words with prefixes have a doubled consonant.
❸ _____ traction	Many metals are drawn toward a magnet.
❹ _____ parition	I thought I saw a ghost! It appeared to me!
❺ _____ cusation	How dare you say I stole your pen!
❻ _____ gression	Too many fights have broken out on the playground lately.
❼ _____ breviation	*Dr.* written before a name means "Doctor." But written after a street name, *Dr.* means "Drive."
❽ _____ celeration	This car can go from 10 miles per hour to 60 miles per hour in 30 seconds.
❾ _____ gravation	No matter how many times I clear the weeds from my flower bed, they keep coming back!
❿ _____ preciation	We want to buy our teacher a card to let her know how much we value what she has done for us.

Name: _____   Date: _____

Read and Reason:
Prefix *ad-* and Its Assimilated Forms

Directions: Read the passages. Circle the words with the prefix *ad-* and its assimilated forms. Then, answer the questions on page 188.

Passage A

Adhesive Tape

In the 1930s, an engineer named Richard Drew worked for 3M. Richard had an appealing idea. He attached an adhesive substance to some cellophane. The result? A product that adhered to surfaces but remained transparent. He knew this invention would be important. So he went to his bosses, whom he called Thrifty Scots. The Thrifty Scots loved the new invention. They called it "Scotch Brand Adhesive Tape®."

3M wanted to advertise this remarkable new product. They needed an aggressive publicity campaign, since no one had ever seen such tape. All the ads featured a cartoon-boy mascot, Scotty McTape, who dressed in a plaid kilt. Scotty solved problems by using tape.

Buyers were attracted to Scotty. Soon everyone started using the phrase "Scotch Tape" as an abbreviation. Today, even when people buy adhesive tape made by other manufacturers, they apply the same name. The name, like the product itself, really sticks!

Read and Reason:
Prefix *ad*- and Its Assimilated Forms *(cont.)*

Passage B

Dear Abby

"Dear Abby" is an advice column that appears in newspapers and online. Pauline Phillips began the column in 1956; her daughter, Jeanne, now writes it. According to its official website, "Dear Abby" is the most admired syndicated column in the world. More than 100 million people read it each day.

The column is meant to entertain and educate. Some teachers use the column to generate classroom discussion on a variety of subjects. Typical topics address relationship problems in people's personal and business lives, alcohol and drug addiction, adversarial relationships, adoption and other children's issues, preventive health, and advocating for volunteerism.

Abby receives more than 10,000 letters and emails per week. More than 80 percent of the correspondence she receives comes from adult readers ages 18 to 49. Many additional letters come from adolescents.

Abby's responses sometimes express admiration and sometimes express sympathy. She often affirms the feelings of her readers, but she occasionally admonishes them. Frequently, she provides additional information to help readers make up their own minds. She addresses each situation on its own and does not adhere to a strict formula. Websites she lists receive many thousands of hits after they are published in a column.

Abby sometimes uses her own common sense to provide advice. Sometimes, others write to refute her responses, and sometimes she admits that her original response to a letter was not adequate.

Abby frequently consults reliable sources to help her craft advice. These have included Supreme Court justices, members of the House of Representatives and Senate, civil rights leaders, respected doctors and scientists, and CEOs of Fortune 500 companies.

"Dear Abby" even has a historical presence. In 1964, the day after Lyndon Johnson's landslide presidential victory, editorial cartoonist Bill Mauldin drew a cartoon captioned "Dear Abby...." The cartoon showed Johnson's defeated opponent Barry Goldwater writing her a letter.

Read and Reason:
Prefix *ad-* and Its Assimilated Forms *(cont.)*

Directions: Read Passage A and respond to the questions below.

❶ Using the words *to, toward* or *add to*, explain what adhesive tape does when it adheres to a surface.

_____

_____

_____

❷ Many words in the passage that begin with the letter *a* followed by a doubled consonant are actually *ad-* words. Explain the meaning of each of the following words by using the words "to, toward, add to":

a. *attractive:* _____

b. *apply:* _____

c. *advertise:* _____

_____

_____

❸ Use the word *adhere* in your own sentence, and explain how the prefix *ad-* means "to, toward or add to":

_____

_____

_____

· ·

Directions: Read Passage B and respond to the questions below.

❶ Why do you think people write to advice columnists like "Dear Abby"?

_____

_____

❷ Do you seek advice from others? Why or why not?

_____

_____

_____

❸ Explain how the words *admire, address,* and *attract* mean "to, toward, add to."

_____

_____

Name: _____   Date: _____

Identify the Prefix and Pick the Best Word

Directions: Circle the best word that completes each sentence below and write it on the line provided. The correct word begins with the prefix indicated within the quotation marks in each sentence. You will repeat some prefixes in your answers.

inter-	between, among
a-, ab-, abs-	away, from, away from
ad- and its assimilated forms	to, toward, add to
di-, dif-, dis-	apart, in different directions; not
super-, sur-	on top of, over, above

1 The harsh dictator threatened to _____ his enemies and to reduce them "to" nothing.
     a. impose   b. interject   c. annihilate   d. abdicate

2 Despite its orderly beginning, the town hall meeting quickly _____into chaos when the mayor refused to answer questions. The meeting fell "apart."
     a. directed   b. dissolved   c. survived   d. abducted

3 Every _____ rises "above" the forces that would destroy him.
     a. detractor   b. interloper   c. superstition   d. survivor

4 I have a strong _____ to crowds. I stay far "away from" them.
     a. attraction   b. abstraction   c. aversion   d. diversion

5 I walked in the rain after catching a cold and _____ my condition. I "added to" my miserable state.
     a. alleviated   b. aggravated   c. alliterated   d. abbreviated

6 Our program will continue after a brief _____. Let's all take a short break "between" segments.
     a. intermission   b. interrogation   c. abdication   d. interjection

7 My thinking was _____ by all the noise that broke my thoughts "apart."
     a. disrupted   b. interfused   c. abstracted   d. superimposed

Prefixes *uni-* and *unit-*

Standards: Uses word origins and derivations to understand word meaning (McREL 2.0)
Uses a variety of sentence structures to expand and embed ideas (McREL 2.3)
Uses conventions of spelling in written compositions (McREL 3.9)
Uses basic elements of structural analysis to decode unknown words (McREL 4.0)
Draws conclusions and makes inferences based on explicit and implicit information in texts (McREL 7.5)

Materials

- *Divide and Conquer: Prefixes uni- and unit-* (page 193)

- *Combine and Create: Prefixes uni- and unit-* (page 194)

- *Read and Reason: Prefixes uni and unit-* (pages 195–197)

Teaching Tips

- This lesson presents the numerical prefixes *uni-* and *unit-*, which mean "one, single." They both attach to intact words (e.g., a *unisex* hair salon; a *unicycle*) and to Latin bases that are not whole words (e.g., *unify, universal).

- This prefix also functions as a base (i.e., as the only root in a word). In such words as *unit, unite, unity,* and *unique,* the prefix is the word's only "semantic unit." When it functions as a base, *uni-, unit-* can also be preceded by another prefix, in such words as *reunite* (to make "one" "again").

- This prefix is found in everyday words (e.g., a military *uniform,* starting a new *unit*), in academic vocabulary (e.g., a *uniform* consistency, a *unilateral* decision, to sing in *unison),*

Teaching Tips *(cont.)*

and in words from Social Studies (*United States, United Nations, unify, unification, labor unions*).

- Some students may initially confuse this prefix with negative *un-* (presented in Unit I, Lesson 3). The Combine and Create exercise provides practice in sorting negative *un-* words from *uni-, unit-* words meaning "one, single."

Guided Practice

Activate Background Knowledge

1. Explain to students that for the next few weeks, they will be looking at words beginning with prefixes of number, size, and quantity, beginning with the number "one."

2. Show students a one-dollar bill and ask, "What do we call a one-dollar bill for short?" Some students will answer "buck," and others will say "a single" or "a one." Accept the answers "single" and "one," and draw an equation on the board: *one (1) = single.*

3. Ask students to think about bicycles. Tell students, "You learned to ride bikes by starting with a tricycle, which has three wheels. Then you advanced to a bicycle, which has two wheels. But in a circus, you might see a clown riding a one-wheeled cycle. What do we call this?" (unicycle). Write the words *unicycle, bicycle,* and *tricycle* on the board, putting a slash in each word before the letter *c* (*uni/cycle, bi/cycle, tri/cycle*). Explain that the three prefixes are numerical. The prefix *uni-* means "one." Present also the form *unit-* = one, single.

Prefixes *uni-* and *unit-* *(cont.)*

Guided Practice *(cont.)* ·············

4. Explain that the first syllable of numerical *uni-* and *unit-* prefixes rhymes with *you*. Write a few more words with the prefixes *uni-* and *unit-* on the board, and have students say them out loud (e.g., *United* States of America, a military *uniform*, a mythical *unicorn*). Ask students, "How do each of these words mean one?" (The *United* States are "one, a single" nation out of many states ["e pluribus unum"]; a *uniform* is a "single" or "one" type of clothing worn by people in a profession; a *unicorn* has a "single, one" horn). If necessary, write the word *unable* on the board. Ask students to pronounce it aloud. Point out that negative *un-* rhymes with *bun*.

5. Explain that in a few words, the prefixes *uni-* and *unit-* may be preceded by *re-* (e.g., *reunion, reunite, reunification*). All these words express the idea of making something "one" "again": in a family *reunion*, relatives come together "again" as a family "unit"; past friends can be *reunited* after a long time, coming together "back, again" and becoming "one"; after a civil war, countries can experience *reunification*, being made "one" "again."

Divide and Conquer

6. Distribute copies of the *Divide and Conquer: Prefixes uni- and unit-* activity sheet (page 193) to students. Guide students through the activity. The practice sheet may be duplicated for each student and/or projected on a projector. Starting with the first word, *unify*, ask, "If the base *fy-* means to 'make, do' and the prefix *uni-* means 'one, single,' then *unify* means to 'make one.' Which definition in the Answer Bank has this meaning?" (The answer is D; to organize into a unit; to consolidate.) Select a few more words from the list and repeat the process.

Combine and Create

7. Distribute copies of the *Combine and Create: Prefixes uni- and unit-* activity sheet (page 194) to students. Ask students to work in pairs to sort the words into the correct columns as negative *un-* words and as *uni-* and *unit-* words meaning "one, single." (Encourage students to pronounce the words out loud.) Review the answers, and ask how the *uni-* and *unit-* words mean "one, single." Also ask students how they distinguished the negative *un-* words (by pronouncing the prefix to rhyme with *bun*). Have them work individually or in pairs to complete the sentences, using four of the words they have written in the left-hand box.

Prefixes *uni-* and *unit-* *(cont.)*

Guided Practice *(cont.)* ·············

Read and Reason

8. Distribute copies of the *Read and Reason: Prefixes uni- and unit-* activity sheets (pages 195–197) to students. Have students read one or both passages and answer the questions. If the passages are too difficult for independent reading, ask students to read in pairs or follow along as you read aloud. Tell them to raise their hands when they hear a word with the *uni-* or *unit-* prefix. Students should circle the words they identify. After you have finished reading, return to the circled words and ask volunteers to explain what they mean. Then, invite students to answer the questions.

> **Extend and Explore**
> Choose from among the activities located on the Teacher Resource CD to give students extra practice with the numerical prefixes *uni-* and *unit-*.

Answer Key ························

Divide and Conquer: Prefixes *uni-* and *unit-* (page 193)

1. unify: one, single; make, do; D
2. uniform: one, single; form, shape; E
3. unilateral: one, single; side; H
4. unison: one, single; sound; F
5. union: one, single; no base; J
6. unique: one, single; no base; C
7. unicorn: one, single; horn; A
8. unicycle: one, single; wheel, circle; G
9. reunion: one, single; union; I
10. united: one, single; no base; B

Combine and Create: Prefixes *uni-* and *unit-* (page 194)

Prefix means "one, single": *unique, universal, unity, unionize, unicolor*

Prefix means "not": *unpopular, unsafe, ungrammatical, uninformed, uninvited*

1. unionize
2. universal
3. unique
4. unity

Read and Reason: Prefixes *uni-* and *unit-* (pages 195–197)

Passage A: *unicorn, universe, uniform, united, unified*

1. Answers will vary. See list above.
2. Answers will vary.

Passage B: *uniforms, union, unanimous, unified, State of the Union, unity, unique, unison, uniformity, unilateral*

1. Answers will vary.
2. Answers will vary.

Name: _____   Date: _____

Divide and Conquer:
Prefixes *uni-* and *unit-*

Directions: Break apart each word below. Write the prefix and its meaning in the first column after the word. In the next column, the base and its meaning are provided. Combine the meanings of the prefix and base and select a definition from the Answer Bank. An example has been done for you.

Answer Bank
A. a mythical animal with a single horn on the forehead
B. organized into a single body; joined together to form a single entity
C. singular; one of a kind; distinctive
D. to organize into a unit; to consolidate
E. always the same, consistent in appearance; also, a consistent type of dress
F. musical agreement; identity of pitch and tone
G. a one-wheeled vehicle propelled by pedals
H. one-sided; affecting or involving only one side or group
I. a gathering of members after a long separation
J. an alliance or organization of two or more people or institutions

word	prefix means	base means	definition
❶ unify	uni- = one, single	fy- = make, do	D
❷ uniform		form- = form, shape	
❸ unilateral		later- = side	
❹ unison		son- = sound	
❺ union		no base	
❻ unique		no base	
❼ unicorn		corn- = horn	
❽ unicycle		cycl- = wheel, circle	
❾ reunion		union	
❿ united		no base	

Name: _____ Date: _____

Combine and Create:
Prefixes *uni-* and *unit-*

Directions: Arrange the words below into their proper boxes. Place five *uni-* or *unit-* words meaning "one, single" in the left-hand box. Place five negative *un-* words in the right-hand box. *Hint:* pronouncing the words out loud will help you distinguish them!

Word Bank				
unpopular	unsafe	unique	uninformed	universal
unity	unionize	unicolor	unicolor	uninvited

Prefix means "one, single"	Prefix means "not"

· ·

Directions: Complete the four sentences by using some of the *uni-* or *unit-* words listed above.

❶ After years of abusive labor practices by the employer, the workers finally voted to

_____ .

❷ The human desire for justice seems to be _____ , ingrained in all human beings throughout the universe.

❸ That poet has a distinctive, even _____ way of expressing himself with words.

❹ We are all in full agreement and have finally achieved _____ of opinion.

Name: _____ Date: _____

Read and Reason:
Prefixes *uni-* and *unit-*

Directions: Read the passages. Circle the words with the prefixes *uni-* and *unit-*. Then, answer the questions on page 197.

Passage A

Unicorn

In the whole of the universe has there ever been born,

a beast as lovely as the unicorn?

As sparkling jewels earthly queens adorn,

this mythical horse wears a single, golden horn.

Its mane suggests not any uniform crown,

but a rainbow of shades cascading down.

Each angle brought together, united in design,

unified in beauty, every single line.

Read and Reason:
Prefixes *uni-* and *unit-* *(cont.)*

Passage B

School Uniform Debate Heats Up

Tempers flared at the Laketown Board of Education meeting Monday night. The topic? Strange as it may sound, the heated debate focused on school uniforms.

Principal Susan Ford outlined the district's stance. "A committee of teachers and administrators has studied this issue for several months," she began. "We read about the advantages and disadvantages of requiring school uniforms. We talked to other districts in our area, both those that have adopted uniforms and those that have not. Faculties in each school voted, and it was discussed at a districtwide teachers' union meeting. Although no vote was unanimous, the vast majority are unified on the issue. We believe uniforms will be an asset to the Laketown Schools."

History teacher Henry Barton spoke next. He reminded the group that President Clinton had first suggested school uniforms in his 1996 State of the Union speech. "Clinton thought uniforms would prevent intruders on campus and reduce gang influences," he said. "Uniforms will promote school unity and minimize differences between wealthier and poorer families."

Several students spoke against requiring uniforms. "Have you *seen* these?" said one. "They are ugly, not at all stylish." "Yes," said another, "I like to be distinctive, even unique, in what I wear!" Many students cried out in unison as they applauded this comment. Another commented, "I think uniforms will end up costing families more. Kids will need two sets of clothes—one for school and one for after school and weekends."

Donald Weems, who represented a "concerned citizens group," also spoke against uniforms. "What's the sense in teaching students to honor diversity and then requiring uniformity in dress?" he queried. An angry parent then interrupted: "Don, you own a clothing shop. Are you really concerned about uniformity? Or are you worried about your sales?" At this point, several audience members began shouting. After several minutes, order was restored.

Board President Hillary Newton closed the meeting by underscoring that the board had no desire to make a unilateral decision. She encouraged those with opinions to email or call her office. The board will vote at its next meeting.

Read and Reason
Prefixes *uni-* and *unit-* (cont.)

Directions: Read Passage A and respond to the questions below.

❶ List five words from the passage that begin with the prefix *uni-* or *unit-*.

_____

_____

_____

_____

❷ The word *uniform* in the passage does not refer to a suit of clothing. Explain how the word *uniform* in this context means "one":

_____

_____

_____

_____

_____

_____

· ·

Directions: Read Passage B and respond to the questions below.

❶ Which arguments do you believe are most compelling? Why?

_____

_____

_____

_____

❷ Do you agree with former President Clinton's stance about school uniforms? Why or why not?

_____

_____

_____

_____

Prefixes *bi-* and *tri-*

Standards: Uses word origins and derivations to understand word meaning (McREL 2.0)
Uses a variety of sentence structures to expand and embed ideas (McREL 2.3)
Uses conventions of spelling in written compositions (McREL 3.9)
Uses basic elements of structural analysis to decode unknown words (McREL 4.0)
Draws conclusions and makes inferences based on explicit and implicit information in texts (McREL 7.5)

Materials

- *Divide and Conquer: Prefixes bi- and tri-* (page 201)

- *Combine and Create: Prefixes bi- and tri-* (page 202)

- *Read and Reason: Prefixes bi- and tri-* (pages 203–205)

Teaching Tips

- This lesson presents two numerical prefixes: *bi-*, meaning "two," and *tri-*, meaning "three." Most students will readily recognize these prefixes from such everyday words as *bicycle*, *bilingual*, *trio*, and *triangle*.

- These prefixes attach to many whole words, as in *bimonthly*, *biweekly*, and *triannual*.

- These prefixes also attach to Latin bases that are not intact words. One of the most important of these bases for social studies is *enni-*, the Latin base for "year": *biennial* elections are held every "two" "years"; *triennial* terms last "three" "years." In geometry, these prefixes attach to the Latin base *sect-*, meaning "cut": we *bisect* an angle by "cutting" it into "two" equal parts; a *trisected* angle has been divided into "three" parts.

Guided Practice

Activate Background Knowledge

1. Show pictures of a unicycle, a bicycle, and tricycle to students. Write the words *bicycle* and *tricycle* on the board, writing a slash before the letter *c* (*bi/cycle*, *tri/cycle*). Ask students what *bi-* means and what *tri-* means.

2. Explain that we use these prefixes to number things. Have students complete these oral sentences: *A camera stand that rests on three legs or feet is called a…* (tripod). Write *tripod* on the board, writing a slash after the letter *i* (*tri/pod*). Then, tell students that the spelling *ped-* is also used for "feet." Explain that a *quadruped* is an animal that walks on "four" "feet." Ask, "What word would describe a creature, such as a human being, who walks on "two" feet?" (*biped*). Write *biped* on the board, writing a slash before the letter *p* (*bi/ped*). Point out that *bi-* and *tri-* words are easy to recognize because they remind us of counting.

3. Tell students that we also use these prefixes to measure and count time and years. Write the Latin base *enni-* on the board, explaining that it means "year." Explain that this base indicates "multiple" years. Write the words *biennial* and *triennial* on the board, and ask which word means "lasting two years or occurring every two years." (*biennial*) Ask which of these words means "lasting three years or occurring every three years"? (*triennial*)

Prefixes *bi-* and *tri-* (cont.)

Guided Practice (cont.) ·············

4. Ask students to work in pairs or groups to brainstorm words they know that use these prefixes. Have them write some of these words on the board and have them explain how they mean "two" or "three" (e.g., *trio, triplets, triathlon, biathlon, bilingual, bifocal, biweekly*). Make sure their answers use the numbers "two" or "three."

Divide and Conquer

5. Distribute copies of the *Divide and Conquer: Prefixes bi- and tri-* activity sheet (page 201) to students. Guide students through the activity. The practice sheet may be duplicated for each student and/or projected on a projector. Starting with the first word, *trisect*, say, "If the base *sect-* means 'to cut' and the prefix *tri-* means 'three,' then *trisect* means 'cut into threes.' Which definition in the Answer Bank has this meaning?" (The answer is E; to divide into three segments or portions.) Select a few more words from the list and repeat the process.

Combine and Create

6. Distribute copies of the *Combine and Create: Prefixes bi- and tri-* activity sheet (page 202) to students. Ask students to work in pairs or individually to match the two-word phrases in Column I with the statements quoted in Column II. When students are done, review the answers, having students read the statements that contain the words *two* or *three*.

Read and Reason

7. Distribute copies of the *Read and Reason: Prefixes bi- and tri-* activity sheets (pages 203–205) to students. Have students read one or both passages and answer the questions. If the passages are too difficult for independent reading, ask students to read in pairs or follow along as you read aloud. Tell them to raise their hands when they hear a word with the prefix *bi-* or *tri-*. Students should circle the words they identify. After you have finished reading, return to the circled words and ask volunteers to explain what they mean. Then invite students to answer the questions.

···································
Extend and Explore
Choose from among the activities located on the Teacher Resource CD to give students extra practice with the numerical prefixes *bi-* and *tri-*.
···································

Prefixes *bi-* and *tri-* (cont.)

Answer Key ·······················

Divide and Conquer: Prefixes *bi-* and *tri-* (page 201)

1. trisect: three; cut; E
2. tripod: three; foot; I
3. biped: two; foot; J
4. bicameral: two; room, chamber; H
5. trilingual: three; language, tongue; F
6. bisect: two; cut; C
7. biennial: two; year; G
8. tricolor: three; color; D
9. biracial: two; race; B
10. trident: three; tooth; A

Combine and Create: Prefixes *bi-* and *tri-* (page 202)

1. C
2. I
3. D
4. J
5. G
6. B
7. A
8. E
9. H
10. F

Read and Reason: Prefixes *bi-* and *tri-* (pages 203–205)

Passage A: *triathlon, bicentennial, biannual, biplane, tri-colored, triathletes, bilingual, binoculars, bicycles*

1. three colors
2. two languages
3. 200 years
4. three events

Passage B: *biennially, biathlon, triathlon, biathletes, bidirectional, bicolored, binoculars, trio, triathletes, bifunctional*

1. Answers will vary.
2. Answers will vary.

Name: _____ Date: _____

Divide and Conquer: Prefixes *bi-* and *tri-*

Directions: Break apart each word below. Write the prefix and its meaning in the first column after the word. In the next column, the base and its meaning are provided. Combine the meanings of the prefix and base and select a definition from the Answer Bank. An example has been done for you.

Answer Bank
A. a three-pronged harpoon or spear
B. consisting of two races
C. to divide into two halves
D. consisting of three colors; triple-hued
E. to divide into three segments or portions
F. speaking three languages
G. occurring every two years; lasting two years
H. consisting of two houses or chambers (as in government)
I. a three-legged stand
J. a creature that walks on two feet

word	prefix means	base means	definition
❶ trisect	tri- = three	sect- = cut	E
❷ tripod		pod- = foot	
❸ biped		ped- = foot	
❹ bicameral		camer- = room, chamber	
❺ trilingual		lingu- = language, tongue	
❻ bisect		sect- = cut	
❼ biennial		enni- = year	
❽ tricolor		color- = color	
❾ biracial		rac- = race	
❿ trident		dent- = tooth	

 201

Name: _____ Date: _____

Combine and Create: Prefixes *bi-* and *tri-*

Directions: If the two-word phrases in Column I could speak, they would match the statements spoken in Column II. Match each phrase with its most appropriate speaker. Every statement includes the word *two* or *three*.

Column I	Column II
❶ _____ bilingual educator	**A.** I am so smart that I can speak three languages.
❷ _____ bilateral agreement	**B.** I am the three-pronged harpoon carried by the Roman god of the sea.
❸ _____ biennial term	**C.** I teach students in two languages: English and Spanish.
❹ _____ bisected angle	**D.** I am an office or position held by a politician for two years at a time.
❺ _____ triennial election	**E.** We offer reduced prices on merchandise two times a year.
❻ _____ Neptune's trident	**F.** The office aide ran three sets of the report to be distributed at the meeting.
❼ _____ trilingual genius	**G.** Voters come to the polls every three years to choose a new mayor.
❽ _____ biannual sales	**H.** The store mails me out every two weeks to collect payment from the customers.
❾ _____ biweekly billing	**I.** Two countries have signed a peace pact establishing the new borders.
❿ _____ triplicate copy	**J.** A geometry student has just cut me in two, from 90 degrees to a double set of 45 degrees.

Name: _____   Date: _____

Read and Reason: Prefixes *bi-* and *tri-*

Directions: Read the passages. Circle the words with the prefixes *bi-* and *tri-*. Then, answer the questions on page 205.

Passage A

A Biannual Competition

Fritz: Greetings, Sports Fans! Welcome to the 200th competition of the Swanville Triathlon!

Don: Does that mean that this is the bicentennial of this event?

Fritz: No, but I am glad you asked. This is a biannual event, so it is completed twice every year. This is the 100th anniversary of the first competition. The festivities are underway. A biplane is flying overhead dragging a tricolored sign of yellow, black, and red. It says, "Congratulations on 100 years! *¡Felicidades por 100 años!*"

Don: Wow! That sign is in English and Spanish. I think it is because so many of our triathletes are bilingual. OK, I am looking through my binoculars now and I can see that the participants are lining up on their bicycles. The race is about to begin!

Read and Reason: Prefixes *bi-* and *tri-* *(cont.)*

Passage B

Two and Three Sports at a Time

The Olympic Games, held biennially with summer and winter games alternating, involve over 13,000 athletes competing in 33 different sports and nearly 400 events. Occasionally, the International Olympic Committee adds new sports to the competitions. The biathlon was added to the winter games in 1960, and the triathlon was introduced during the summer games in 2000.

Biathlon describes any sporting event made up of two disciplines, but the term usually refers to a combination of rifle shooting and cross-country skiing. The sport began as military training for Norwegian soldiers, during which biathletes ski around a cross-country track and carry rifles. The total distance is broken up by shooting rounds, half in prone position, the other half standing. For each shooting, the biathlete must hit five targets. The targets are bidirectional and bicolored; they turn from black to white when they are hit. This helps both athletes and spectators with their binoculars keep track of progress. Depending on the shooting performance, extra distance or time is added to the contestant's total. As in most races, the winner has the shortest total time.

A *triathlon* involves a trio of continuous and sequential endurance events. Although variations exist, the most popular form of the triathlon involves swimming, cycling, and running. Triathletes compete for fastest overall course-completion time, including timed transitions between the individual components.

The swim leg usually proceeds around a series of marked buoys in open water. Racers leave the water, enter the transition area, and prepare for cycling. Cyclers ride around a marked course, typically on public roads, and end at the transition area, where they rack their bicycles and prepare for the running stage. The entire triathlon ends at a finish line near the transition area.

Training for these endurance events is intense. In most cases, athletes cross-train. This bifunctional training, necessary for these sports, is often safer than training for a single activity. The Olympic motto is *Citius, Altius, Fortius*, a Latin expression that means "Faster, Higher, Stronger." This motto applies to both biathletes and triathletes.

Read and Reason: Prefixes *bi-* and *tri-* (cont.)

Directions: Read Passage A and respond to the questions below.

❶ How many colors does the tricolored sign have?

_____

_____

❷ How many languages does someone who is bilingual speak?

_____

_____

❸ How many years are celebrated in a bicentennial anniversary?

_____

_____

❹ How many events are there in a triathlon?

_____

_____

• •

Directions: Read Passage B and respond to the questions below.

❶ Do you think competing in a triathlon would be more difficult than competing in one of the three events alone? Why or why not?

_____

_____

_____

_____

❷ Why do you think bifunctional training is safer than training for a single activity?

_____

_____

_____

_____

Prefixes *quart-, quadr-, deca-, decim-, cent(i)-,* and *mill(i)-*

Standards: Uses word origins and derivations to understand word meaning (McREL 2.0)
Uses a variety of sentence structures to expand and embed ideas (McREL 2.3)
Uses conventions of spelling in written compositions (McREL 3.9)
Uses basic elements of structural analysis to decode unknown words (McREL 4.0)
Draws conclusions and makes inferences based on explicit and implicit information in texts (McREL 7.5)

⋯ Materials

- *Divide and Conquer:* Prefixes *quart-, quadr-, deca-, decim-, cent(i)-* and *mill(i)-* (page 210)

- *Combine and Create:* Prefixes *quart-, quadr-, deca-, decim-, cent(i)-* and *mill(i)-* (page 211)

- *Read and Reason:* Prefixes *quart-, quadr-, deca-, decim-, cent(i)-* and *mill(i)-* (pages 212–214)

⋯ Teaching Tips

- This lesson presents the numerical prefixes for 4, 10, 100, and 1,000. These prefixes indicate either whole numbers (100 years in a *century*, 4 feet on a *quadruped)* or fractions (a *quarter* is $\frac{1}{4}$ of a dollar, a *centigram* is $\frac{1}{100}$ of a gram).

- All these prefixes are Latin except for the form *deca-*, which is Greek. The prefix *deca-* is always pronounced with a "hard *c*" (e.g., *decagon, decahedron*) and refers to multiples of 10. The Latin prefix *decim-* is pronounced with a "soft *c*" (e.g., *decimal, decimate*) and refers to fractions of $\frac{1}{10}$.

⋯ Teaching Tips *(cont.)*

- These prefixes attach to Latin and Greek bases that are not intact words. One of the most important of these bases for social studies vocabulary is *enni-*, the Latin base for "year": the United States President is elected for a *quadrennial* term that lasts "four" "years"; *centennial* celebrations are held every "100" "years"; a *millennium* lasts "1,000" "years." The prefixes for 100 and 1,000, furthermore, may be preceded by other numerical prefixes: *bicentennial* (200 years), *tricentennial* (300 years), etc.

- These prefixes appear in words from mathematics. In Geometry, students learn that *quadrilateral* figures are "four" "sided"; a *decagon* (hard *c*) is a polygon with "10" sides or "angles"; a *decimal* point (soft *c*) indicates $\frac{1}{10}$. Words like *centigram, milligram, decaliter,* and *millimeter* appear in the metric system.

- Some interesting facts about number words: the word *mile* is from Latin *mille*: it was originally the length of 1,000 paces as marched by a Roman soldier. Today, a mile consists of 5,280 feet. In England, stones were set into the ground, marking distances between towns: these are called *milestones*. We also use the word *milestone* to indicate a significant event in our life that marks "how far we have come." The word *million* is also Latin, meaning "1,000 × 1,000" (a thousand thousands). The verb *decimate* means "to randomly destroy a large portion," as in "The tornado *decimated* the downtown area."

Prefixes *quart-, quadr-, deca-, decim-, cent(i)-,* and *mill(i)-* (cont.)

Guided Practice ·················

Activate Background Knowledge

1. Show students real or play money coins and bills. Explain that today they will learn four more numerical prefixes for the numbers 4, 10, 100, and 1,000.

2. Give one student a one-dollar bill. Ask, "How many quarters must I give you to make an equal exchange for your dollar?" (The answer is 4.) Give the student four quarters and take the dollar back. Write the word *quarter* on the board, slashing it after the letter *t* (*quart/er*). Write *quart- = four* on the board. Ask, "If I divide a gallon into four equal parts, what have I made?" (The answer is quarts.) Explain that there are four quarts in a gallon and four quarters in a dollar because *quart-* means four.

3. Write the form *quadr-* on the board, explaining that *quadr-* is another form of this numerical prefix. Draw a rectangle and count the sides: explain that this figure is a *quadrilateral*. Remind students that in the previous lesson, they learned the word *biped* for a person who walks on "two" "feet." Ask, "What would I call a horse or dog that moves on four feet?" (The answer is *quadruped*.)

4. Write the number *1.5* on the board. Circle the decimal point and ask, "What do we call this point or dot? What does it mean?" (The answer is $\frac{1}{10}$.) Write the following on the board: *decim- = 10* and *deca- = 10*. Pronounce both prefixes correctly: *decim-* with a soft *c*, *deca-* with a hard *c*. Have students practice. Ask, "If a hexagon has six sides, what would I call a polygon with 10 sides or angles?" (The answer is *decagon*.)

5. Give the dollar bill to another student. Ask, "How many pennies must I give you to make an equal exchange for your dollar?" (The answer is 100.) Write the following on the board: *100 cents = 1 dollar*. Explain that the prefix *cent- = 100*. Ask, "How many years are in a century?" (The answer is 100.) Say, "There are 100 cents in a dollar and 100 years in a century because *cent-* means 100."

6. Write *mill(i)- = 1,000* on the board and ask, "Who knows a word with this prefix?" Students may answer, "Millionaire." Follow up by asking, "How many dollars are in a million dollars?" (The answer is 1,000 x 1,000.) Tell them that the Romans measured "miles" in sets of 1,000 steps marched by a soldier. Explain that the prefix *mill(i)-* is also used for very small quantities of $\frac{1}{1000}$, as in *milligram*. Ask, "If a meter contains 100 centimeters, how many millimeters does it contain?" (The answer is 1,000.)

Prefixes *quart-, quadr-, deca-, decim-, cent(i)-,* and *mill(i)-* *(cont.)*

Guided Practice *(cont.)* ·············

Divide and Conquer

7. Distribute copies of the *Divide and Conquer: Prefixes quart-, quadr-, deca-, decim-, cent(i)-* and *mill(i)-* activity sheet (page 210) to students. Guide students through the activity. The practice sheet may be duplicated for each student and/or projected on a projector. Starting with the first word, *quadruped,* ask, "If the base *ped-* means 'foot' and the prefix *quadr-* means 'four,' then *quadruped* means 'four-footed.' Which definition in the Answer Bank has this meaning?" (The answer is E; four-footed; a creature that moves on four legs.) Select a few more words from the list and repeat the process.

Combine and Create

8. Distribute copies of the *Combine and Create: Prefixes quart-, quadr-, deca-, decim-, cent(i)-* and *mill(i)-* activity sheet (page 211) to students. Ask students to work individually or in pairs to complete the words by adding the correct forms of the numerical prefixes. Upon completion, ask students to read their answers (including definitions) aloud. Ask them to explain the number that each word refers to.

Read and Reason

9. Distribute copies of the *Read and Reason: Prefixes quart-, quadr-, deca-, decim-, cent(i)-* and *mill(i)-* activity sheets (pages 212–214) to students. Have students read one or both passages and answer the comprehension questions. If the passages are too difficult for independent reading, ask students to read in pairs or follow along as you read aloud. Tell them to raise their hands when they hear a word with these numerical prefixes. Students should circle the words they identify. After you have finished reading, return to the circled words and ask volunteers to explain what they mean. Then invite students to answer the questions.

:···:
: **Extend and Explore**   :
: Choose from among the   :
: activities located on the Teacher   :
: Resource CD to give students   :
: extra practice.   :
:···:

Prefixes *quart-*, *quadr-*, *deca-*, *decim-*, *cent(i)-*, and *mill(i)-* *(cont.)*

Answer Key ························

Divide and Conquer: Prefixes *quart-*, *quadr-*, *deca-*, *decim-*, *cent(i)-*, and *mill(i)-* (page 210)

1. quadruped: four; foot; E
2. decagon: ten; angle; J
3. centennial: hundred; year; G
4. quadrennial: four; year; B
5. millennium: thousand; year; A
6. bicentennial: two; hundred; year; D
7. milliliter: thousand; liter; I
8. quadrilateral: four; side; H
9. decimal: ten; no base; C
10. quarter: four; no base; F

Combine and Create: Prefixes *quart-*, *quadr-*, *deca-*, *decim-*, *cent(i)-*, and *mill(i)-* (page 211)

1. quartet
2. century
3. milligram
4. decimal
5. decapod
6. centigram
7. decaliter
8. centurion
9. cents
10. quarts

Read and Reason: Prefixes *quart-*, *quadr-*, *deca-*, *decim-*, *cent(i)-*, and *mill(i)-* (pages 212–214)

Passage A: *quadricentennial, quart, centigrade, quarter, quarters, quadrant, cent*

1. 400; *quadr-* means "four" and *centi-* means "hundred"
2. one
3. 100; *cent(i)-* means 100, and boiling occurs at 100 degrees, or "grades" of temperature

Passage B: *quadrants, millennium, centurions, centuries, centennial, quadratic, decimals, quad, quadrangle, millionaire, quadrupeds, centipede, millipede, quarterfinals*

1. Answers will vary.
2. Answers will vary, but can include scientists describe insects with more legs than can easily be counted *centipedes*, perhaps rounding to a large number.

Name: _____   Date: _____

Divide and Conquer: Prefixes *quart-, quadr-, deca-, decim-, cent(i)-,* and *mill(i)-*

Directions: Break apart each word below. Write the prefix and its meaning in the first column after the word. In the next column, the base and its meaning are provided. Combine the meanings of the prefix and base and select a definition from the Answer Bank. An example has been done for you.

Answer Bank
A. a period of 1,000 years
B. lasting four years or occurring every four years
C. a point between numbers indicating $\frac{1}{10}$
D. a 200th-year celebration
E. four-footed; a creature that moves on four legs
F. $\frac{1}{4}$; also, a 25-cent piece
G. a 100th-year celebration
H. consisting of four sides
I. $\frac{1}{1000}$ of a liter (liquid measure)
J. a polygon with 10 sides

	word	prefix means	base means	definition
1	quadruped	quadr(u)- = four	ped- = foot	E
2	decagon		gon- = angle	
3	centennial		enni- = year	
4	quadrennial		enni- = year	
5	millennium		enni- = year	
6	bicentennial		enni- = year	
7	milliliter		liter- = liter	
8	quadrilateral		later- = side	
9	decimal		no base	
10	quarter		no base	

Name: _____   Date: _____

Combine and Create: Prefixes *quart-,* *quadr-, deca-, decim-, cent(i)-,* and *mill(i)-*

Directions: Write the correct form of the numerical prefix to generate the number words described in each sentence.

Number word	Sentence
1 _____ et	We have one soprano, one alto, one tenor, and one bass in our singing group.
2 _____ ury	I am 100 years long.
3 _____ gram	1,000 of me make up a total gram.
4 _____ al	My dot or point indicates $\frac{1}{10}$ of the number.
5 _____ pod	I am a crustacean, such as a crab or lobster, with 10 feet protruding from my main body.
6 _____ gram	100 of me make up a total gram.
7 _____ liter	I am a liquid measure totaling 10 liters.
8 _____ urion	I am an officer in the Roman army in charge of 100 soldiers.
9 _____ s	100 of me make a whole dollar.
10 _____ s	Four of me make a gallon.

Name: _____ Date: _____

Read and Reason: Prefixes *quart-, quadr-, deca-, decim-, cent(i)-, and mill(i)-*

Directions: Read the passages. Circle the words with the prefixes *quart-, quadr-, deca-, decim-, cent(i)-,* and *mill(i)-*. Then, answer the questions on page 214.

Passage A

Quadricentennial Cookie Pie Recipe

Our European town is celebrating its quadricentennial this year! Make this pie to celebrate!

Ingredients:

- I quart each strawberry, blueberry, vanilla, and chocolate ice cream, softened
- I package cookie dough in a tube

Directions:

Preheat the oven to 200 degrees centigrade (because we live in Europe, we use the metric system).

Press the cookie dough into a pie crust. Bake for one quarter of an hour. Let it cool. Imagine the crust is divided into four wedge-shaped quarters. Press one flavor of ice cream into each quadrant. Rechill pie in the freezer.

To serve:

Place entire pie on the table. Try to give each guest a sliver from each quadrant. Just for fun, charge one cent per piece in honor of what it might have cost when our town was first founded.

Read and Reason: Prefixes *quart-*, *quadr-*, *deca-*, *decim-*, *cent(i)-*, and *mill(i)-* *(cont.)*

Passage B

Dear Diary,

Last week, my parents and I accompanied my brother on college visits. We spent a day at a small school and another day at the state university. On each campus, we did a lot of walking around and even attended some classes. My brother is trying to decide on a major as well as the size of the college, so we had lots to do on each campus.

The small school had only four main buildings. These were used to establish "quadrants," one for math and science, another for English and foreign languages, a third for social sciences, and the fourth for fine arts. We attended an ancient history lecture in the social science building and heard about Bronze Age people living in the second millennium BC. We also heard about ancient Roman armies and the centurions who commanded the battalions. The Roman Empire, we learned, endured for several centuries. In the fine arts building, we heard a chorus preparing for the school's upcoming centennial celebration. I peeked in on a math class and saw a quadratic equation on the whiteboard and even some decimals—finally, something I was familiar with!

In the middle of the state university campus was a large, grassy rectangle called the quad, short for quadrangle. The quad was several city blocks in length. The student union was at one end and athletic buildings were at the other. Along both sides were six to eight large buildings. We toured a museum in the zoology building, which a millionaire alumnus had endowed. One room featured life-sized sculptures of quadrupeds, some as small as squirrels and others as large as elephants. Another room displayed insects and other arthropods. I liked this exhibit because I like bugs. Did you know that the centipede doesn't necessarily have 100 legs? It can have as few as 34 or as many as 354! Of course, millipedes don't have 1,000 legs; their bodies have 20–100 segments with a pair of legs per segment.

Since my brother likes sports, we walked through the basketball arena and stumbled upon a pep rally! The team was headed to the quarterfinals of a tournament. The noise level of the shouting was so high that we couldn't hear ourselves talk! This was a good, peppy way to end our visit.

Read and Reason: Prefixes *quart-, quadr-, deca-, decim-, cent(i)-,* and *mill(i)-* (cont.)

Directions: Read Passage A and respond to the questions below.

❶ How many years are celebrated in a *quadricentennial*? How do you know?

_____

_____

_____

❷ If each quart of ice cream is one quarter of a gallon, how many total gallons of ice cream are required to make this pie?

_____

❸ On a centigrade thermometer, water freezes at a temperature of zero. At what temperature, on the same thermometer, does water come to a boil? How do you know?

_____

_____

_____

• •

Directions: Read Passage B and respond to the questions below.

❶ Since centipedes do not necessarily have 100 legs, how do you suppose they got their name?

_____

_____

_____

❷ Which college do you think the boy should select? Why?

_____

_____

_____

Quantitative Prefixes
multi- and *poly-*

Standards: Uses word origins and derivations to understand word meaning (McREL 2.0)
Uses a variety of sentence structures to expand and embed ideas (McREL 2.3)
Uses conventions of spelling in written compositions (McREL 3.9)
Uses basic elements of structural analysis to decode unknown words (McREL 4.0)
Draws conclusions and makes inferences based on explicit and implicit information in texts (McREL 7.5)

Materials

- *Divide and Conquer: Prefixes multi- and poly-* (page 218)

- *Combine and Create: Prefixes multi- and poly-* (page 219)

- *Read and Reason: Prefixes multi- and poly-* (pages 220–222)

Teaching Tips

- This lesson presents the Latin prefix *multi-* and the Greek prefix *poly-*, both of which mean "many." These prefixes appear in many academic words.

- Most students will readily recognize the prefix *multi-* from such words as *multiply*, *multiplex*, and *multivitamin*.

- The prefix *poly-* appears in many content area words: *polytheism* (belief in "many" gods), *polygraph* (lie detector which records "many" bodily responses, such as pulse, breathing, and temperature), and *polygon* (geometric figure with "many" angles and sides).

Teaching Tips *(cont.)*

- In everyday speech and in the commercial world of advertising, the prefix *multi-* often attaches to already existing words to create clever neologisms (new words) to attract customer attention.

- Though long and "polysyllabic," words beginning with these prefixes are relatively easy to Divide and Conquer. As students identify the prefixes, they should ask themselves, "How does this word mean 'many'?"

- **Note:** In the word *monopoly*, the prefix *mono-* means "only, one"; the base *poly-* means "sale, sell" and is not connected with the prefix *poly-*. A *monopoly* is exclusive ownership of a market by someone who is the "only" "seller."

- These prefixes do not assimilate.

Guided Practice

Activate Background Knowledge

1. Write the word *multiply* on the board, followed by *2 x 3 = 6*, *3 x 3 = 9* and *4 x 3 = 12*. Ask students, "When I *multiply*, what do I do with the number?" (You increase it or add it many times.) Write *multi- = many* on the board. Ask students to work with partners and brainstorm other *multi-* words. Record their answers on the board and ask them to explain how each *multi-* word means "many." Answers may include such actual words as *multivitamin*, *multitalented*, *multimillionaire*, and *multimedia*.

Quantitative Prefixes *multi-* and *poly-* *(cont.)*

Guided Practice *(cont.)* ·············

2. Draw a few *polygons* on the board (e.g., rectangle, hexagon, octagon). Demonstrate that *polygons* are *multilateral* because they have *many* sides. Explain the prefix *poly-* is Greek, meaning "many." Say, "The ancient Greeks believed in 'many' 'gods.' If the Greek base for *god* is *the-*, can you compose the word describing their religion?" (The answer is *polytheism*; the ancient Greeks were *polytheistic*.)

3. Demonstrate that *poly-* words tend to be long and polysyllabic. Write the word *polysyllabic* on the board, writing a slash after the letter *y* (*poly/syllabic*). Ask, "Who can explain what this word means?" Point out how easy the word is to understand after identifying the prefix. Show students that, by dividing the prefix from the rest of the word, they can easily divide and conquer academic words like *polygamy* (multiple marriages), *Polynesia* (many islands), and even *polyphony* (many sounds or voices).

Divide and Conquer

4. Distribute copies of the *Divide and Conquer: Prefixes multi-* and *poly-* activity sheet (page 218) to students. Guide students through the activity. The sheet may be duplicated for each student and/or projected on a projector. Starting with the first word, *polytheism*, ask, "If the base *the-* means 'god' and the prefix *poly-* means 'many,' then *polytheism* means 'many gods.' Which definition in the Answer Bank has this meaning?" (The answer is B; belief in many gods or deities.) Select a few more words from the list and repeat the process.

Combine and Create

5. Distribute copies of the *Combine and Create: Prefixes multi-* and *poly-* activity sheet (page 219) to students. Ask students to work individually or in pairs to complete the sentences and to compose their own sentences using any *multi-* or *poly-* word of their choice (including those in the word bank). Invite students to read their sentences aloud. Then discuss how each *multi-* and *poly-* word in their sentences means "many."

Quantitative Prefixes *multi-* and *poly-* (cont.)

Guided Practice *(cont.)* ·············

Read and Reason

6. Distribute copies of the *Read and Reason: Prefixes multi-* and *poly-* activity sheets (pages 220–222) to students. Have students read one or both passages and answer the comprehension questions. If the passages are too difficult for independent reading, ask students to read in pairs or follow along as you read aloud. Tell them to raise their hands when they hear a word with the prefixes *multi-* or *poly-*. Circle the words they identify. After you have finished reading, return to the circled words and ask volunteers to explain what they mean. Then, invite students to answer the questions.

> **Extend and Explore**
> Choose from among the activities located on the Teacher Resource CD to give students extra practice.

Answer Key ·····················

Divide and Conquer: Prefixes *multi-* and *poly-* (page 218)

1. polytheism: many; god; B
2. multipartite: many; part; A
3. multicolored: many; color; J
4. polygamist: many; marry; F
5. multilingual: many; language, tongue; I
6. polysyllabic: many; syllable; C
7. multitude: many; state, quality (suf.); D
8. polygon: many; angle; G
9. multipy: many; fold; H
10. multidimensional: many; dimension; E

Combine and Create: Prefixes *multi-* and *poly-* (page 219)

1. multiple
2. polysyllabic
3. multiplex
4. polytechnic
5. multitude
6. multilingual

Sentences will vary.

Read and Reason: Prefixes *multi-* and *poly-* (pages 220–222)

Passage A: *multifaceted, polytechnic, multiplication, polygons, multicultural, multilingual, multitude*

1. Answers will vary. For *multifaceted*, accept a wide range of responses expressing many subjects, variety of course, many different activities, different applications, etc.
2. Answers will vary. For *polygon*, accept a wide range of geometric figures (e.g., triangle, rectangle, square, rhombus, trapezoid, pentagon, octagon, decagon).
3. Answers will vary. For *multilingual*, accept responses expressing the idea of many languages, languages spoken by people from different countries, etc.

Passage B: *multitasking, multitask, multitude, multiple, multimedia, multiples, polysyllabic, polygons, multitaskers*

1. Answers will vary.
2. Answers will vary.

Name: _____   Date: _____

Divide and Conquer:
Prefixes *multi-* and *poly-*

Directions: Break apart each word below. Write the prefix and its meaning in the first column after the word. In the next column, the base and its meaning are provided. Combine the meanings of the prefix and base and select a definition from the Answer Bank. An example has been done for you.

Answer Bank
A. consisting of many parts
B. belief in many gods or deities
C. extremely long (of words); consisting of three or more syllables
D. a crowd or throng; a large mass
E. consisting of many dimensions; complex
F. one who engages in multiple marriages at the same time
G. a many-sided geometric figure or shape
H. to increase or make manifold; to reproduce
I. polyglot; speaking many languages
J. consisting of many colors

word	prefix means	base means	definition
❶ polytheism	poly- = many	the- = god	B
❷ multipartite		part- = part	
❸ multicolored		color- = color	
❹ polygamist		gam- = marry	
❺ multilingual		lingu- = language, tongue	
❻ polysyllabic		syllab- = syllable	
❼ multitude		-tude = state, quality (suf.)	
❽ polygon		gon- = angle	
❾ multiply		ply- = fold	
❿ multidimensional		dimension- = dimension	

Name: _____   Date: _____

Combine and Create:
Prefixes *multi-* and *poly-*

Directions: Below are some academic words beginning with the prefixes *multi-* and *poly-*. In the sentences below, use each of these words as a substitute for the words and phrases in parentheses. Then, compose two sentences using your own *multi-* and/or *poly-* words. You may select your favorite two words from the list, or you may compose your own!

Word Bank		
polysyllabic	multitude	multiple
multiplex	multilingual	polytechnic

❶ I have told you _____ (many) times to look both ways when crossing the street!

❷ The teacher liked to show off by using _____ (long) words when shorter ones would have said the same thing.

❸ We decided to go to the _____ (theater showing many different films at the same time) so that each of us could see what he or she wanted.

❹ Because he wanted to become an engineer, he decided to apply to a _____ (specializing in many different technologies and sciences) university.

❺ The speaker's voice could hardly be heard over the roar of the _____ (crowd).

❻ With her _____ (singing in many languages) talent for singing in French, Spanish, English, and Greek, the entertainer had fans across the world.

My two sentences using words beginning with multi- and/or poly- are:

_____

_____

_____

_____

_____

_____

_____

_____

Name: _____   Date: _____

Read and Reason:
Prefixes *multi-* and *poly-*

Directions: Read the passages. Circle the words with the prefixes *multi-* and *poly-*. Then, answer the questions on page 222.

Passage A

A Parent's Decision

We knew that finding a new school for our children was not going to be easy. Education is important to us. We had definite ideas about good schooling. A multifaceted perspective was important. We wanted the children to learn many different things from many different points of view. We looked at the polytechnic school. It was strong in math and science. It even had separate courses in multiplication, division, and polygons! But we were looking for more.

We looked for a multicultural environment. We wanted the children to learn about people from many places. In fact, we wanted them to learn one or more foreign languages and become multilingual.

In the end, we chose the World Academy. Students at the World Academy come from many lands. The school has a multitude of subjects for students. We believe that our children will be happy at this school.

Read and Reason:
Prefixes *multi-* and *poly-* (cont.)

Passage B

Multitasking

Do you multitask? Multitasking is the handling of more than one task (from two to a multitude) at the same time. For example, playing a computer game while talking on the phone is multitasking. Some believe that multitasking is necessary in our increasingly technological society. Others believe that multitasking impairs our ability to focus and concentrate. Multiple news reports have emerged reporting the dangers of driving a car while multitasking.

Some psychologists study the nature, limits, and effects of multitasking. Their studies have revealed multiple findings. In general, they find that people are easily distracted when as few as two very simple tasks are performed at the same time, especially if both tasks require making a decision or selecting a particular action. Other researchers have studied multitasking in specific domains, such as learning. Even in multimedia learning, it was found that people find it difficult, almost impossible, to learn new information if they are engaged in multitasking that takes their attention away from the lesson.

People have a limited ability to absorb and retain information. This problem multiplies when the amount of information increases. People also require meaningful contexts to assist them in memorization. If you were given a random string of polysyllabic words to remember in succession, for example, you might try to make the words memorable by inventing a story that contains them or by creating phrases with the words. Likewise, if you were to recall a sequence of polygons in random order (hexagon, decagon, octagon, triangle, quadrangle), you would need time to form a picture of each figure in your mind. Without multiple strategies like these, all of which require time and focused concentration, your brain is capable only of storing a limited amount of information in its short-term memory.

Rapidly increasing technology fosters multitasking because it promotes multiple sources of input at a given time. According to studies by the Kaiser Family Foundation, multitasking while using media increased from 10 percent to 26 percent from 1999 to 2005. One-quarter to one-third of people also do something else "most of the time" while watching TV, listening to music, or reading. As technology provides more distractions, attention is spread among tasks more thinly.

Some research suggests that the human brain can be trained to multitask. One study discovered that the brain's ability to deal with competing information develops until the mid-teens. Perhaps if people are trained to multitask at an early age, they will become efficient multitaskers. More research is needed.

Read and Reason:
Prefixes *multi-* and *poly-* *(cont.)*

Directions: Read Passage A and respond to the questions below.

❶ Given the context of the word, explain how a *multifaceted* education means "many."

_____

_____

_____

❷ Explain how *polygon* means many. Name at least three different kinds of polygons.

_____

_____

_____

❸ Given the context of the word, explain what *multilingual* means.

_____

_____

_____

- -

Directions: Read Passage B and respond to the questions below.

❶ Do you multitask? If so, why? If not, why not?

_____

_____

_____

❷ Many communities are banning talking on the phone while driving, a form of multitasking. What do you think about these rules?

_____

_____

More Quantitative Prefixes *magn(i)-*, *mega-*, *megal(o)-*, and *micro-*

Standards: Uses word origins and derivations to understand word meaning (McREL 2.0)
Uses a variety of sentence structures to expand and embed ideas (McREL 2.3)
Uses conventions of spelling in written compositions (McREL 3.9)
Uses basic elements of structural analysis to decode unknown words (McREL 4.0)
Draws conclusions and makes inferences based on explicit and implicit information in texts (McREL 7.5)

Materials

- *Divide and Conquer:* Prefixes *magn(i)-*, *mega-*, *megal(o)-*, and *micro-* (page 227)

- *Combine and Create:* Prefixes *magn(i)-*, *mega-*, *megal(o)-*, and *micro-* (page 228)

- *Read and Reason:* Prefixes *magn(i)-*, *mega-*, *megal(o)-*, and *micro-* (pages 229–231)

Teaching Tips

- This lesson presents the Latin prefix *magn(i)-* and the Greek prefixes *mega-* and *megal(o)-*, meaning "big, large, great." This lesson also presents the Greek prefix *micr(o)-*, meaning "small."

- Students may already know many words beginning with these prefixes: *megachurch, megasale, megabucks* are readily recognized as meaning "big, large, great." In its combined form, the prefix *mega-* is written as *megal(o)-* in such words as *megalopolis,* and *megalomania.* Because modern technology promotes "small" devices, the prefix *micr(o)-* is readily recognized in such words as *microphone, microchip,* and *microscope.*

Teaching Tips *(cont.)*

- The Latin prefix *magn(i)-* appears in important academic words, such as the *magnitude* of an earthquake (its "large" scope and ranking on the Richter Scale), the *Magna Carta* (the "great" charter of civil liberties), and the *magnum opus* (the "great" work) of a composer, artist, or writer.

- *Spelling Note:* These prefixes afford an excellent opportunity for students to learn an important spelling pattern in words based on Greek and Latin roots. In words with multiple Greek roots, the vowel *o* is used as a connector: *microscope, microfiber, megalopolis, megalomaniac.* When students meet a long technical word, they should look for the "connecting *o*" and divide and conquer at that point. In words with multiple Latin roots, by contrast, the connecting vowel is *i*: *magnificent, magnitude, magnify.*

- These prefixes do not assimilate.

Guided Practice

Activate Background Knowledge

1. Roll a sheet of construction paper into a cone, hold it to your mouth, and speak through it. Ask students if they know the name for this cone (*megaphone*). Ask volunteers to explain what a *megaphone* does to your voice (makes your voice louder, bigger, and greater).

More Quantitative Prefixes *magn(i)-, mega-, megal(o)-,* and *micro-* *(cont.)*

Guided Practice *(cont.)* ·············

2. Write the word *megaphone* on the board, writing a slash after the letter *a* (*mega/phone*). Write *mega-* = *big, large, great* on the board. Write the form *megal(o)-* on the board, explaining that this is another form of the prefix. Ask, "If the Greek word for *city* is *polis*, what do I call a "large city"?" (*megalopolis*) Write *megalopolis* on the board, and divide around the connecting *o* (*megalo/polis*). Explain that all words beginning with *mega-* and *megal(o)-* mean "big, large, great."

3. Ask students to work with partners to create their own *mega-* and *megal(o)-* words. Ask them to write their words on the board and describe how they mean "big." Answers might include a mix of actual and made-up words (e.g., *megabucks, megastore, megaburger, megatruck, megasale*).

4. Pretend to hold a spyglass to your eye. Ask students if they can think of another prefix (Latin) that also means "big." Ask, "What do I call this lens that makes things 'big' so that I can see them better?" (*magnifying* lens) Write *magnify* on the board, dividing around the connecting *i* (*magni/fy*). Write *magn(i)-* = *big, large, great* on the board. Ask students, "What would I call a really great party, using a word beginning with *magn(i)-*?" (*magnificent*) Explain that many words beginning with *magn(i)-* also mean "big, large, great." Sample words are *magnitude*, a business *magnate*, and the *Magna Carta*.

5. Ask students what the opposite of *big* is (small). Write *micr(o)-* = *small* on the board. Explain that *micr(o)-* is the opposite of *mega-*. Ask students to work individually or with partners to generate actual or made-up words of opposite meaning that begin with *mega-, megal(o)-* and *micro-*. Ask them to write some of their words on the board and explain how they mean "big" or "small." Examples might include: *microwave* oven vs. *megawave* oven, *microscope* vs. *megascope, megaphone* vs. *microphone* (both make a "small" "voice" "louder, greater"), a *megadose* of medicine vs. a *microdose*.

Divide and Conquer

6. Distribute copies of the *Divide and Conquer: Prefixes magn(i)-, mega-, megal(o)-,* and *micro-* activity sheet (page 227) to students. Guide students through the activity. The practice sheet may be duplicated for each student and/or projected on a projector. Starting with the first word, *megalith*, ask, "If the base *lith-* means 'stone' and the prefix *mega-* means 'big, large, great,' then a *megalith* is a 'big stone.' Which definition in the Answer Bank has this meaning?" (The answer is G; a huge stone used to build ancient monuments.) Select a few more words from the list and repeat the process.

More Quantitative Prefixes *magn(i)-,* *mega-, megal(o)-,* and *micro-* (cont.)

Guided Practice (cont.)

Combine and Create

7. Distribute copies of the *Combine and Create: Prefixes magn(i)-, mega-, megal(o)-,* and *micro-* activity sheet (page 228) to students. Ask students to work individually or in pairs to sort the words according to their prefixes as "big" or "small" words and to match the "big" words with their imaginary speakers.

Read and Reason

8. Distribute copies of the *Read and Reason: Prefixes magn(i)-, mega-, megal(o)-,* and *micro-* activity sheets (pages 229–231) to students. Have students read one or both passages and answer the questions. If the passages are too difficult for independent reading, ask students to read in pairs or follow along as you read aloud. Tell them to raise their hands when they hear a word that contains any of the quantifying prefixes. Students should circle the words they identify. After you have finished reading, return to the circled words and ask volunteers to explain what they mean. Then, invite students to answer the questions.

> **Extend and Explore**
> Choose from among the activities located on the Teacher Resource CD to give students extra practice.

Answer Key

Divide and Conquer: Prefixes *magn(i)-, mega-, megal(o)-,* and *micro-* (page 227)

1. megalith: big, great, large; stone; G
2. microscope: small; look at, examine; J
3. magnate: big, great, large; no base; D
4. magnitude; big, great, large; state or quality; E
5. megalomania: big, great, large; madness; H
6. megalopolis: big, great, large; city; A
7. microcosm: small; world; I
8. megaphone: big, great, large; voice, sound; B
9. magnify: big, great, large; do, make; C
10. megadose: big, great, large; give; F

Combine and Create: Prefixes *magn(i)-, mega-, megal(o)-,* and *micro-* (page 228)

Prefix means "big, large, great": *megalomaniac, megapower, Magna Carta, magnum opus, megabucks, magnificent, magnitude, megastore*

Prefix means "small": *microfibers, microchip, microscopic, microfilm*

1. magnum opus
2. Magna Carta
3. megalomaniac
4. magnitude
5. megapower

More Quantitative Prefixes *magn(i)-*, *mega-*, *megal(o)-*, and *micro-* (cont.)

Answer Key (cont.) ··················

Read and Reason: Prefixes *magn(i)-*, *mega-*, *megal(o)-*, and *micro-* (pages 229–231)

Passage A: *magnifying, microscope, microscopic, magnified, microcosm, microbes, megalomaniac, megalopolis, magnificent*

1. Answers will vary. Accept responses explaining that a microscope enables us to see very small objects. It is used to study tiny specimens, very small samples, etc.

2a. megalopolis

2b. megalomaniac

2c. magnificent

3. Sentences will vary.

Passage B: *magnificent, megaliths, magnitude, microscopic, microanalysis, microorganisms, microscopes*

1. Answers will vary.

2. Answers will vary.

Count Me! (page 232)

1. E

2. A

3. G

4. B

5. J

6. H

7. D

8. C

9. F

10. I

Name: _____   Date: _____

Divide and Conquer: Prefixes *magn(i)-, mega-, megal(o)-, and micro-*

Directions: Break apart each word below. Write the prefix and its meaning in the first column after the word. In the next column, the base and its meaning are provided. Combine the meanings of the prefix and base and select a definition from the Answer Bank. An example has been done for you.

Answer Bank
A. a very large urban area
B. cone used to magnify the voice
C. to enlarge
D. a person of important rank or power; a "big shot"
E. size, extent, or quantity
F. a very large dose of medication
G. a huge stone used to build ancient monuments
H. excessive fondness for grandiose performance; fantasies of great wealth and power
I. a small representative example of a larger system or operation
J. an optical instrument used to enlarge minute objects

	word	prefix means	base means	definition
❶	megalith	mega- = big, large, great	lith- = stone	G
❷	microscope		scop- = look at, examine	
❸	magnate		no base	
❹	magnitude		-(i)tude = state or quality	
❺	megalomania		mania- = madness	
❻	megalopolis		polis- = city	
❼	microcosm		cosm- = world	
❽	megaphone		phon- = voice, sound	
❾	magnify		fy- = do, make	
❿	megadose		dos- = give	

Name: _____   Date: _____

Combine and Create: Prefixes *magn(i)-, mega-, megal(o)-,* and *micro-*

Directions: Examine the prefixes and phrases below and rewrite them in the correct boxes as "big" or "small" words. Then, select words from the left-hand box to match the statements by the imaginary speakers at the bottom of the page.

Word Bank					
megalomaniac	microfibers	megapower	microchip	microfilm	microscopic
magnum opus	megabucks	magnificent	Magna Carta	megastore	magnitude

Prefix means "big, large, great"	Prefix means "small"

❶ _____ I am Beethoven's Ninth Symphony, considered by many to be his greatest work.

❷ _____ I am the Great Charter of Civil Liberties granted by King John in 1215.

❸ _____ I am a person who loves to show off with my huge houses and fancy cars. I think I have megabucks!

❹ _____ I am the scope or extent of an earthquake, as measured by a seismograph.

❺ _____ I am a nation with a lot of money and a huge military. Other nations fear and respect me.

Name: _____   Date: _____

Read and Reason: Prefixes *magn(i)-,* *mega-, megal(o)-, and micro-*

Directions: Read the passages. Circle the words with the prefixes *magn(i)-, mega-, megal(o)-* and *micro-*. Then, answer the questions on page 231.

Passage A

The Size of Things

Have you ever thought about the size of things? Find a magnifying glass. Or, even better, look through a microscope. A single drop of pond water can contain thousands of microscopic life forms. A single drop of water, when magnified, can be seen as a microcosm of life on Earth. To the microbes in the water, we might appear as huge as the sun! It is enough to make a person feel overly important. But just when you start to feel like a megalomaniac, think again. Consider a megalopolis like New York City or London. These magnificent cities extend for miles. And yet, they are tiny when compared to even the smallest ocean. Then, look up. Each spot of light is a star like our sun. Now it is our turn to feel microscopic!

Read and Reason: Prefixes *magn(i)-, mega-, megal(o)-,* and *micro-* (cont.)

Passage B

The Magnificent Mystery of Stonehenge

Stonehenge is a magnificent prehistoric monument located in the English countryside. It is composed of earthworks, which are artificial changes in land levels surrounding a circular setting of megaliths, or large standing stones. Archaeologists believe that the monument was erected around 2,500 BC in several construction phases that lasted at least 1,500 years.

The magnitude of Stonehenge construction is impressive. Archaeologists believe that builders first dug two concentric holes in the center of the site. The holes held up to 80 standing stones, only 43 of which can be traced today. Scientists believe the stones came from an area of Wales about 160 miles away. Each monolith measures around $6\frac{1}{2}$ feet in height, between $3\frac{1}{2}$ and 5 feet in width, and about $2\frac{1}{2}$ feet thick. The northeastern entrance to the monument precisely matches the direction of the midsummer sunrise and midwinter sunset of the period. Despite the enormous size of the megaliths, they are arranged with an almost microscopic precision!

Scientists use microanalysis and other techniques to understand how Stonehenge was constructed. The work of these researchers has been impeded by such factors as soil erosion, animal burrowing, other natural disturbances, and by the poor quality of later records that refer to the site. Deer and ox bones, flint tools, Roman coins, and medieval artifacts have been found at the site. An excavation held between 2003 and 2008 discovered microorganisms from 7000 BC, so the site may be even older than originally thought.

Several theories about Stonehenge's purpose have been suggested. The most prominent one suggests that it was a domain of the dead, connected to a nearby town by the River Avon. According to this interpretation, a journey along the Avon to reach Stonehenge was part of a ritual passage from life to death, an observance made by the living to honor long-dead ancestors and the recently deceased.

Stonehenge was produced by a culture that left no written records. Many aspects of its construction and use are still subject to debate. For example, how did workers transport stones of such magnitude from so far away? How were workers able to set entrances in the directions of sunrise and sunset in an age that had no telescopes or microscopes? What was the purpose of the monument? These and other questions contribute to the "magnificent mystery of Stonehenge."

Read and Reason: Prefixes *magn(i)-,* *mega-, megal(o)-,* and *micro-* (cont.)

Directions: Read Passage A and respond to the questions below.

❶ Using the word *small*, explain what a *microscope* does.

_____

_____

_____

❷ Find the words in the passage that have these meanings:

a. a vastly large city or urban area: _____

b. a person who thinks he is a big shot, fantasizing about his own importance and greatness:

_____

c. grand and splendid, wonderful, making a big impression: _____

❸ Use the word *microscope* in a sentence of your own.

_____

_____

· ·

Directions: Read Passage B and respond to the questions below.

❶ Why do you think Stonehenge has captivated people's imaginations for such a long time?

_____

_____

_____

❷ What role might a microanalysis play in understanding the mysteries of Stonehenge?

_____

_____

_____

Name: _____   Date: _____

Count Me!

Directions: If the words and two-word phrases in Column I could speak, they would match the statements spoken in Column II. Match each word or phrase with its most appropriate speaker. Every statement includes a numerical word (two, three, four, ten) or a word of size and quantity (much, many, large) that indicates the prefix of the correct match.

Column I	Column II
1 _____ quadrilateral polygon	**A.** I am a belief system that worships many gods.
2 _____ polytheistic religion	**B.** I am the two-hundred year anniversary of a historic town.
3 _____ magnifying lens	**C.** There is no one like me, because I am one of a kind, a singular being.
4 _____ bicentennial celebration	**D.** I am an international contract reflecting the many sides of the countries who have signed me.
5 _____ bicameral legislature	**E.** I am a rectangle, square, parallelogram, rhombus, or trapezoid. I am any four-sided geometric figure.
6 _____ triple decker	**F.** I am a bacterium or protozoan of extremely small size.
7 _____ multilateral agreement	**G.** A crime investigator uses me to make tiny fingerprints seem large.
8 _____ unique individual	**H.** I am a three-story bus; I am also a tall sandwich with three slices of bread.
9 _____ microorganism	**I.** The commander in chief made me without consulting with anyone else: I am totally one-sided.
10 _____ unilateral decision	**J.** I consist of two rooms or chambers within the government: the Senate and the House of Representatives.

References Cited

Baumann, J., Carr-Edwards, E., Font, G., Tereshinski, C., Kame'enui E., and Olejnik, S. 2002. Teaching morphemic and contextual analysis to fifth-grade students. *Reading Research Quarterly* 37: 150–176.

Baumann, J.F., Font, G., Edwards, E.C., and Boland, E. 2005. *Strategies for teaching middle-grade students to use word-part and context clues to expand reading vocabulary.* In E.H. Hiebert & M.L. Kamil eds., *Teaching and learning vocabulary: Bringing research to practice,* 179–205. Mahwah, NJ: Erlbaum.

Bear, D., Invernizzi, M., Templeton, S., and Johnston, F. 2007. *Words their way* 4th ed. Upper Saddle River, NJ: Prentice Hall.

Beck, I.L., McKeown, M.G., and Kucan, L. 2002. *Bringing words to life: Robust vocabulary instruction.* New York: Guilford.

Beck, I., Perfetti, C., and McKeown, M. 1982. Effects of long-term vocabulary instruction on lexical access and reading comprehension. *Journal of Educational Psychology* 74: 506–521.

Biemiller, A. 2005. Size and sequence in vocabulary development: Implications of choosing words for primary grade vocabulary. In E.H. Hiebert & M.L. Kamil eds., *Teaching and learning vocabulary: Bringing research to practice,* 223–242. Mahwah, NJ: Erlbaum.

Biemiller, A., and Slonim, N. 2001. Estimating root word vocabulary growth in normative and advantaged populations: Evidence for a common sequence of vocabulary acquisition. *Journal of Educational Psychology* 93: 498–520.

Blachowicz, C.L.Z., and Fisher, P. 2006. *Teaching vocabulary in all classrooms,* 3rd ed. Upper Saddle River, NJ: Pearson/Merrill/Prentice Hall.

Blachowicz, C.L.Z., Fisher, P.J.L., Ogle, D., and Watts-Taffe, S. 2006. Vocabulary: Questions from the classroom. *Reading Research Quarterly* 41(4): 524–538.

Carlisle, J. 2000. Awareness of the structure and meaning of morphologically complex words: Impact on reading. *Reading and writing: An Interdisciplinary Journal* 12: 169–190.

Carlisle, J. 2010. Effects of instruction in morphological awareness on literacy achievement: An integrative review. *Reading Research Quarterly* (45): 464–487.

Cunningham, P. 2004. *Phonics they use: Words for reading and writing.* New York: Longman.

Fuchs, D. and Fuchs, L.S. 1998. Treatment validity: A unifying concept for reconceptualizing the identification of learning disabilities. *Learning Disabilities Research and Practice,* 13(4), 204–219.

Graves, M.F. and Watts-Taffe, S.M. 2002. The place of word consciousness in a research-based vocabulary program. In A.E. Farstrup & S.J. Samuels eds., *What research has to say about reading instruction,* 140–165. Newark, DE: International Reading Association.

References Cited *(cont.)*

Harmon, J.M., Hedrick, W.B., and Wood, K.D. 2005. Research on vocabulary instruction in the content areas: Implications for struggling readers. *Reading & Writing Quarterly* (21): 261–280.

Kame'enui, E., Carnine, D., and Freschi, R. 1982. Effects of text construction and instructional procedures for teaching word meanings on comprehension and recall. *Reading Research Quarterly* 17: 367–388.

Kieffer, M., and Lesaux, N. 2007. Breaking down words to build meaning: Morphology, vocabulary, and reading comprehension in the urban classroom. *The Reading Teacher* 61: 134–144.

Lehr, F., Osborn, J., and Hiebert, E.H. 2007. Research-based practices in early reading series: A focus on vocabulary. Available from http://www.prel.org/products/re_/ES0419.htm.

Mountain, L. 2005. ROOTing out meaning: More morphemic analysis for primary pupils. *The Reading Teacher* 58: 742–749.

Nagy, W.E., Anderson, R.C., Schommer, M., Scott, J.A., and Stallman, A. 1989. Morphological families in the internal lexicon. *Reading Research Quarterly* (24): 262–282.

Nagy, W.E., and Scott, J.A. 2000. Vocabulary processes. In *Handbook of reading research, Vol. III*, eds. M. L. Kamil, P. B. Mosentahl, P. D. Pearson, and R. Barrm 269–284. Mahwah, NJ: Erlbaum.

National Association of State Directors of Special Education (NASDE). 2006. *Response to intervention: Policy considerations and implementation*. Alexandria, VA: NASDE, Inc.

Porter-Collier, I. M. 2010. *Teaching vocabulary through the roots approach in order to increase comprehension and metacognition.* Unpublished Master's degree project. Akron, OH: University of Akron.

Rasinski, T. and Padak, N. 2008. *From phonics to fluency*, 2nd ed. New York: Longman.

Rasinski, T., Padak, N., Newton, R., and Newton, E. 2008. *Greek and Latin roots: Keys to building vocabulary*. Huntington Beach, CA: Shell Education.

Stahl, S. and Fairbanks, M. 1986. The effects of vocabulary instruction: A model-based meta-analysis. *Review of Educational Research* 56: 72–110.

Contents of the Teacher Resource CD

page	title	filename
26	Divide and Conquer: Two-Syllable Compound Words	dctwosyllable.pdf
27	Combine and Create: Two-Syllable Compound Words	cctwosyllable.pdf
28–30	Read and Reason: Two-Syllable Compound Words	rrtwosyllable.pdf
34	Divide and Conquer: Three-Syllable Compound Words	ddthreesyllable.pdf
35	Combine and Create: Three-Syllable Compound Words	ccthreesyllable.pdf
36–38	Read and Reason: Three-Syllable Compound Words	rrthreesyllable.pdf
41	Divide and Conquer: Negative Prefix *un-*	dcnegprefixun.pdf
42	Combine and Create: Negative Prefix *un-*	ccnegprefixun.pdf
43–45	Read and Reason: Negative Prefix *un-*	rrnegprefixun.pdf
49	Divide and Conquer: Negative Prefix *in-*	dcnegprefixin.pdf
50	Combine and Create: Negative Prefix *in-*	ccnegprefixin.pdf
51–53	Read and Reason: Negative Prefix *in-*	rrnegprefixin.pdf
57	Divide and Conquer: Negative Prefixes *im-* and *il-*	dcnegprefixesimil.pfg
58	Combine and Create: Negative Prefixes *im-* and *il-*	ccnegprefixesimil.pdf
59–61	Read and Reason: Negative Prefixes *im-* and *il-*	rrnegprefixesimil.pdf
62	What a Negative Predicament!	negpredicament.pdf
66	Divide and Conquer: Prefix *re-*	dcprefixre.pdf
67	Combine and Create: Prefix *re-*	ccprefixre.pdf
68–70	Read and Reason: Prefix *re-*	rrprefixre.pdf
74	Divide and Conquer: Prefix *pre-*	dcprefixpre.pdf
75	Combine and Create: Prefix *pre-*	ccprefixpre.pdf
76–78	Read and Reason: Prefix *pre-*	rrprefixpre.pdf
82	Divide and Conquer: Prefixes *ex-*, *e-*, and *ef-*	dcprefixesexeef.pdf
83	Combine and Create: Prefixes *ex-*, *e-*, and *ef-*	ddprefixesexeef.pdf
84–86	Read and Reason: Prefixes *ex-*, *e-*, and *ef-*	rrprefixesexeef.pdf
90	Divide and Conquer: Prefix *sub-* and Its Assimilated Forms	dcprefixsubandforms.pdf
91	Combine and Create: Prefix *sub-* and Its Assimilated Forms	ccprefixsubandforms.pdf
92–94	Read and Reason: Prefix *sub-* and Its Assimilated Forms	rrprefixsubandforms.pdf
98	Divide and Conquer: Prefixes *co-* and *con-*	dcprefixescocon.pdf
99	Combine and Create: Prefixes *co-* and *con-*	ccprefixescocon.pdf
100–102	Read and Reason: Prefixes *co-* and *con-*	rrprefixescocon.pdf

Contents of the Teacher Resource CD *(cont.)*

page	title	filename
103	Picking the Best Prefix	pickingbestprefix.pdf
107	Divide and Conquer: Prefixes *in-*, *im-*, and *il-*	ddprefixesinimil.pdf
108	Combine and Create: Prefixes *in-*, *im-*, and *il-*	ccprefixesinimil.pdf
109–111	Read and Reason: Prefixes *in-*, *im-*, and *il-*	rrprefixesinimil.pdf
115	Divide and Conquer: Prefixes *com-* and *col-*	ddprefixescomcol.pdf
116	Combine and Create: Prefixes *com-* and *col-*	ccprefixescomcol.pdf
117–119	Read and Reason: Prefixes *com-* and *col-*	rrprefixescomcol.pdf
123	Divide and Conquer: Prefix *de-*	dcprefixde.pdf
124	Combine and Create: Prefix *de-*	ccprefixde.pdf
125–127	Read and Reason: Prefix *de-*	rrprefixde.pdf
131	Divide and Conquer: Prefix *pro-*	dcprefixpro.pdf
132	Combine and Create: Prefix *pro-*	ccprefixpro.pdf
133–135	Read and Reason: Prefix *pro-*	rrprefixpro.pdf
140	Divide and Conquer: Prefixes *trans-* and *tra-*	dcprefixestranstra.pdf
141	Combine and Create: Prefixes *trans-* and *tra-*	ccprefixestranstra.pdf
142–144	Read and Reason: Prefixes *trans-* and *tra-*	rrprefixestranstra.pdf
145	Name that Direction!	namedirection.pdf
150	Divide and Conquer: Prefix *inter-*	dcprefixinter.pdf
151	Combine and Create: Prefix *inter-*	ccprefixinter.pdf
152–154	Read and Reason: Prefix *inter-*	rrprefixinter.pdf
159	Divide and Conquer: Prefixes *di-*, *dif-*, and *dis-*	dcprefixesdidifdis.pdf
160	Combine and Create: Prefixes *di-*, *dif-*, and *dis-*	ccprefixesdidifdis.pdf
161–163	Read and Reason: Prefixes *di-*, *dif-*, and *dis-*	rrprefixesdidifdis.pdf
167	Divide and Conquer: Prefixes *a-*, *ab-*, and *abs-*	dcprefixesaababs.pdf
168	Combine and Create: Prefixes *a-*, *ab-*, and *abs-*	ccprefixesaababs.pdf
169–171	Read and Reason: Prefixes *a-*, *ab-*, and *abs-*	rrprefixesaababs.pdf
175	Divide and Conquer: Prefixes *super-* and *sur-*	dcprefixessupersur.pdf
176	Combine and Create: Prefixes *super-* and *sur-*	ccprefixessupersur.pdf
177–179	Read and Reason: Prefixes *super-* and *sur-*	rrprefixessupersur.pdf
184	Divide and Conquer: Prefix *ad-* and Its Assimilated Forms	dcprefixadandforms.pdf
185	Combine and Create: Prefix *ad-* and Its Assimilated Forms	ccprefixadandforms.pdf

Contents of the Teacher Resource CD (cont.)

page	title	filename
186–188	Read and Reason: Prefix *ad-* and Its Assimilated Forms	rrprefixadandforms
189	Identify the Prefix and Pick the Best Word	identifyprefixpickbest.pdf
193	Divide and Conquer: Prefixes *uni-* and *unit-*	dcprefixesuniunit.pdf
194	Combine and Create: Prefixes *uni-* and *unit-*	ccprefixesuniunit.pdf
195–197	Read and Reason: Prefixes *uni-* and *unit-*	rrprefixesuniunit.pdf
201	Divide and Conquer: Prefixes *bi-* and *tri-*	dcprefixesbitri.pdf
202	Combine and Create: Prefixes *bi-* and *tri-*	ccprefixesbitri.pdf
203–205	Read and Reason: Prefixes *bi-* and *tri-*	rrprefixesbitri.pdf
210	Divide and Conquer: Prefixes *quart-*, *quadr-*, *deca-*, *decim-*, *cent(i)-*, and *mill(i)-*	dcprefixesquarttomilli.pdf
211	Combine and Create: Prefixes *quart-*, *quadr-*, *deca-*, *decim-*, *cent(i)-*, and *mill(i)-*	ccprefixesquarttomilli.pdf
212–214	Read and Reason: Prefixes *quart-*, *quadr-*, *deca-*, *decim-*, *cent(i)-*, and *mill(i)-*	rrprefixesquarttomilli.pdf
218	Divide and Conquer: Prefixes *multi-* and *poly-*	dcprefixesmultipoly.pdf
219	Combine and Create: Prefixes *multi-* and *poly-*	ccprefixesmultipoly.pdf
220–222	Read and Reason: Prefixes *multi-* and *poly-*	rrprefixesmultipoly.pdf
227	Divide and Conquer: Prefixes *magn(i)-*, *mega-*, *megal(o)-*, and *micro-*	dcprefixesmagnitomicro.pdf
228	Combine and Create: Prefixes *magn(i)-*, *mega-*, *megal(o)-*, and *micro-*	ccprefixesmagnitomicro.pdf
229–231	Read and Reason: Prefixes *magn(i)-*, *mega-*, *megal(o)-*, and *micro-*	rrprefixesmagnitomicro.pdf
232	Count Me!	countme.pdf

Additional Resources	filename
Extend and Explore	extendexplore.pdf
Scattergories Matrix	scattergoriesmatrix.pdf
Wordo Matrix	wordomatrix.pdf
Word Pyramid	wordpyramid.pdf
Word Spokes	wordspokes.pdf
Prefixes Flashcards	prefixesflashcards.pdf

Notes